Rupert Brooke
& Wilfred Owen

Selected and edited by GEORGE WALTER

University of Sussex

WEIDENFELD & NICOLSON

First published in 1997 by Everyman Paperbacks
This edition published in 2023 by Weidenfeld & Nicolson
An imprint of The Orion Publishing Group Ltd
Carmelite House
50 Victoria Embankment
London
EC4Y 0DZ

An Hachette UK Company

1 3 5 7 9 10 8 6 4 2

A CIP catalogue record for this book is available from the British Library.

ISBN mmp: 978 1 3996 1406 1
ISBN ebook: 978 1 3996 1407 8

Printed in the UK by Clays Ltd, Elcograf S.p.A.

www.orionbooks.co.uk
www.weidenfeldandnicolson.co.uk

Contents

Note on the Authors and Editor   vi
Chronology of Brooke's and Owen's Lives and Times   viii
Introduction   xviii
Note on the Text   xxiii

RUPERT BROOKE

1914 and Other Poems   3

1914
I. Peace   3
II. Safety   4
III. The Dead   5
IV. The Dead   6
V. The Soldier   7
The Treasure   8

The South Seas
Tiare Tahiti   9
Retrospect   12
The Great Lover   14
Heaven   17
Doubts   18
There's Wisdom in Women   19
He wonders whether to praise or to blame her   20
A Memory   21
One Day   22
Waikiki   23
Hauntings   24
Sonnet (suggested by some of the Proceedings
  of the Society for Psychical Research)   25
Clouds   26

Mutability   27

Other Poems
The Busy Heart   29
Love   30
Unfortunate   31
The Chilterns   32
Home   34
The Night Journey   35
Song   36
Beauty and Beauty   37
The Way that Lovers use   38
Mary and Gabriel   39
The Funeral of Youth: Threnody   41

Grantchester
The Old Vicarage, Grantchester   43

Other Related Poems   47

Fafaïa   47
A Song   48
Fragment   49

WILFRED OWEN   51

Poems by Wilfred Owen   53

Preface   53
Strange Meeting   54
Another Version   55
Greater Love   56
Apologia pro Poemate Meo   57
The Show   59
Mental Cases   61
Parable of the Old Men and the Young   62
Arms and the Boy   63
Anthem for Doomed Youth   64

The Send-off 65
Insensibility 66
Dulce et Decorum est 68
The Sentry 69
The Dead-Beat 71
Exposure 72
Spring Offensive 74
The Chances 76
S. I. W. 77
Futility 79
Smile, Smile, Smile 80
Conscious 81
A Terre 82
Wild with all Regrets 84
Disabled 86
The End 88

Other Related Poems 89

Song of Songs 89
The Next War 90
Miners 91
Hospital Barge 93
Asleep 94

Notes 95
Glossary of Slang and Military Terms Used by Owen 103

Note on the Authors and Editor

RUPERT BROOKE was born in Rugby in 1887. The son of a housemaster at Rugby School, he was educated there and was still at school when his earliest poems were published under a variety of aliases. He was an undergraduate at King's College, Cambridge between 1906 and 1910 and his first book of verse, *Poems*, appeared in 1911. Two years later, he became a Fellow of King's and then embarked upon a year-long journey around America and the South Seas. Joining the Royal Naval Division when war broke out, he saw action in Antwerp but contracted septicaemia from a mosquito bite whilst en route to Gallipoli and died on St George's Day, 1915. He was buried on the island of Scyros and the impact of his death upon public consciousness ensured that the posthumously published *1914 and Other Poems* became an immediate bestseller.

WILFRED OWEN was born in Oswestry in 1893, the eldest son of a railway official. He was educated at the Birkenhead Institute and Shrewsbury Technical School and first began to write poetry seriously as a teenager. In 1911, he failed the London University matriculation examination and became an unpaid lay assistant in an evangelical parish at Dunsden. Two years later, after failing to win a scholarship to University College, Reading he moved to France to become an English teacher. He returned to England in 1915 and, in the following year, fought on the Somme with the Manchester Regiment. Invalided home in 1917 with shell-shock, he was a patient at Craiglockhart War Hospital where he became friends with Siegfried Sassoon. He was awarded the Military Cross shortly after his return to the Western Front in 1918, and was killed on the Oise-Sambre canal a week before the war ended. Only five of his poems appeared in print during his lifetime but posthumous editions of his work, such as *Poems by Wilfred Owen* published in 1920, established his reputation as one of the finest poets of his generation.

GEORGE WALTER is a Lecturer in English in the School of Cultural and Community Studies at the University of Sussex. His other publications include *Ivor Gurney: Best Poems and the Book of Five Makings* (MidNAG & Carcanet, 1995) with R. K. R. Thornton and *Ivor Gurney: Selected Poems* (Everyman, 1996).

Chronology of Brooke's and Owen's Lives

Year	Ages	Lives
1887		Rupert Chawner Brooke born 3 August in Rugby; second of three sons of William Parker Brooke, a housemaster at Rugby School, and Mary Cotterill
1893		Wilfred Edward Salter Owen born in Plas Wilmot, Oswestry; eldest of four children of Tom Owen, a railway official, and Susan Shaw
1897	10	Brooke attends Hillbrow Preparatory School, Rugby
	4	Owen family move to Birkenhead

Chronology of Their Times

Year	Literary Context	Historical Events
1887	Conan Doyle, *A Study in Scarlet*	Queen Victoria's Golden Jubilee
1888		Jack the Ripper murders in Whitechapel; County councils set up in Britain
1889	Stevenson, *The Master of Ballantrae* Swinburne, *Poems and Ballads*	
1890	Wilde, *The Picture of Dorian Gray*	First underground railway in London
1891	Hardy, *Tess of the D'Urbervilles*	
1892	Death of Tennyson Kipling, *Barrack-Room Ballads*	
1893	John Davidson, *Fleet Street Eclogues* Francis Thompson, *Poems*	Independent Labour Party formed
1894	Shaw, *Arms and the Man*	Gladstone resigns as prime minister over Irish Home Rule
1895	Wilde, *The Importance of Being Earnest* Yeats, *Poems*	Marconi's 'wireless' telegraphy; Freud publishes first work on psychoanalysis
1896	Alfred Austin becomes Poet Laureate Housman, *A Shropshire Lad*	
1897	James, *What Maisie Knew* Stoker, *Dracula*	Queen Victoria's Diamond Jubilee; Revolt on Indian North-West Frontier

Year	Ages	Lives
1900	7	Owen attends Birkenhead Institute
1901	14	Brooke attends Rugby School as member of his father's house
1905	18	Brooke's first published poem, 'Sicilian Octave', appears in *The Westminster Gazette* under the pseudonym Sandro
1906	19	Brooke wins scholarship to read Classics at King's College, Cambridge
1907	20	Brooke helps to found Marlowe Society for performance of Renaissance drama. Begins to publish poems under his own name
1908	21	Brooke becomes friends with Edward Marsh
	15	Owen family move to Shrewsbury. Owen attends Shrewsbury Technical School
1909	22	Brooke becomes President of the Cambridge University Fabian Society. Awarded a Second in his Classical Tripos and so switches to English Literature for his final year. Wins Charles Oldham Shakespeare Scholarship.
1910	23	Brooke's father dies of a brain haemorrhage and Brooke temporarily takes over his duties at Rugby. Wins Harness Prize for essay on Puritanism in Elizabethan drama. Spends summer touring south-west speaking on Poor Law reform on behalf of Fabians. Moves to Old Vicarage, Grantchester in December
1911	24	Brooke travels on continent for five months, staying in Munich and Florence. Works on dissertation on John Webster for Fellowship at King's on his return. *Poems* published in December

Year	Literary Context	Historical Events
1898	Wells, *The War of the Worlds* Hardy, *Wessex Poems*	Death of Gladstone; Curies discover radium
1899		Boer War begins
1900	Death of John Ruskin	Boxer Rebellion in China
1901	Kipling, *Kim*	Death of Queen Victoria and accession of Edward VII
1902	Bennett, *Anna of the Five Towns*	Boer War ends
1903	Butler, *The Way of All Flesh*	Wright brothers make first powered air flight
1904	Barrie; *Peter Pan*	
1905	W. H. Davies, *The Soul's Destroyer and Other Poems*	Emmeline Pankhurst founds Women's Social and Political Union
1906	Galsworthy, *The Man of Property*	First Labour MPs
1908	Chesterton, *The Man Who Was Thursday* Hardy, *The Dynasts*	
1909	Death of Swinburne Forster, *Howards End*	Old Age Pension introduced; Blériot flies across English Channel
1910	Yeats, *Responsibilities and Other Poems*	Death of Edward VII and accession of George V; Post-Impressionist exhibition in London
1911	Masefield, *The Everlasting Mercy*	Liberal Government introduces national unemployment and medical insurance; Amundsen reaches South Pole

Year	Ages	Lives
	18	Owen works as a pupil-teacher at Wyle Cop School, Shrewsbury, whilst studying for University of London matriculation exam. Fails to matriculate and takes unpaid position as lay assistant and pupil of the Reverend Herbert Wigan at Dunsden, an evangelical parish near Reading
1912	25	Brooke suffers nervous breakdown and convalesces in Cannes and Munich. Returns to Germany for two months in April and lives in Berlin. Conceives *Georgian Poetry* with Edward Marsh, Harold Monro and Wilfrid Gibson
	19	Owen attends classes in English and Botany at University College, Reading. Experiences at Dunsden provoke crisis of faith
1913	26	Brooke awarded Fellowship at King's. Travels to America in May and explores America and Canada before moving on to Samoa and Fiji. Invited to contribute to *New Numbers* project by Wilfrid Gibson and Lascelles Abercrombie. Spends December in New Zealand
	20	Owen abandons evangelical religion and leaves Dunsden suffering from physical and mental illness. Fails scholarship exam for University College, Reading and moves to Bordeaux in September to teach English at Berlitz School
1914	27	Brooke spends four months in Tahiti, returning to England in June. Commissioned in the Royal Naval Division in September and takes part in unsuccessful Antwerp expedition. Joins Hood Battalion at Blandford for training in December
	21	Owen becomes tutor to the Léger family in the High Pyrenees, meeting the symbolist poet Laurent Tailhade there. Returns to Bordeaux in September to become freelance English teacher. Accepts post as private tutor to the de la Touche family at Mérignac in December

Year	Literary Context	Historical Events
1912	*Georgian Poetry 1911–1912* de la Mare, *The Listeners*	Loss of the *Titanic*
1913	Robert Bridges becomes Poet Laureate First issue of *New Numbers* Lawrence, *Sons and Lovers*	Panama Canal opens
1914	*Des Imagistes* anthology Robert Frost, *North of Boston*	Outbreak of First World War; Battles of Mons and the Marne Antwerp expedition

Year	Ages	Lives
1915	27	Hood Battalion sail for the Dardanelles in February. Brooke contracts acute septicaemia from a mosquito bite and dies at Scyros on 23 April. Leaves royalties to Wilfrid Gibson, Lascelles Abercrombie and Walter de la Mare in his will. *1914 and Other Poems* published in June
	22	Owen returns to England in September and enlists in Artists' Rifles. Stationed in Essex for rest of year
1916	23	Owen commissioned as Second Lieutenant in Manchester Regiment in June. Makes unsuccessful attempt to transfer to Royal Flying Corps. Arrives in France on 29 December
1917	24	Owen joins Manchester Regiment on Somme front. Evacuated to 13th Casualty Clearing Station at Gailly in March with concussion and again in May with shell-shock. Returns to England and is sent to Craiglockhart War Hospital for treatment. Becomes editor of the hospital magazine, *The Hydra*, which prints his first published poem, 'Song of Songs'. Begins friendship with Siegfried Sassoon and gains acceptance in literary circles. Passed fit for home service by Medical Board in October and rejoins Manchester Regiment at Scarborough. Promoted to Lieutenant
1918		*Collected Poems of Rupert Brooke: With a Memoir* published
	25	Owen stationed at Ripon before returning to Scarborough in June. Returns to France in August and is awarded Military Cross in October after successful action in Beaurevoir-Fonsomme line. Killed by machine gun fire on Oise-Sambre canal on 4 November
1920		*Poems by Wilfred Owen* published
1921		Revised edition of *Poems by Wilfred Owen* published

Year	Literary Context	Historical Events
1915	Buchan, *The Thirty-Nine Steps* Wilfrid Gibson, *Battle*	Battle of Neuve Chapelle; Gallipoli campaign; Loss of the *Lusitania*
1916	Henri Barbusse, *Le Feu* Jessie Pope, *Simple Rhymes for Stirring Times*	Battles of Verdun and the Somme; Irish revolt
1917	Sassoon, *The Old Huntsman and Other Poems* Graves, *Fairies and Fusiliers* Laurence Binyon, *For the Fallen and Other Poems*	Battle of Passchendaele; Russian Revolution; America enters First World War
1918	Sassoon, *Counter-Attack and Other Poems* Hopkins, *Poems* Wyndham Lewis, *Tarr*	Battle of Arras; German offensive on Somme: First World War ends
1919	*Wheels 1919: A Fourth Cycle*	Treaty of Versailles; Alcock and Brown fly across Atlantic
1920	Edward Thomas, *Collected Poems* Pound, *Hugh Selwyn Mauberley*	First meeting of League of Nations
1921		Irish Free State founded

Year	Ages	Lives

1928   New edition of *Collected Poems of Rupert Brooke: With a Memoir* published

1931   *The Poems of Wilfred Owen: Edited with a Memoir by Edmund Blunden* published

Year	Literary Context	Historical Events
1922	T. S. Eliot, *The Waste Land* Joyce, *Ulysses* Isaac Rosenberg, *Poems* Edmund Blunden, *The Shepherd and Other Poems of Peace and War*	Mussolini comes to power after march on Rome
1924		First Labour Government in Britain
1925	Woolf, *Mrs Dalloway*	
1926		The General Strike
1928	Edmund Blunden, *Undertones of War* Sassoon, *Memoirs of a Fox-Hunting Man*	British women win equal voting rights with men
1929	Graves, *Good-bye to All That* R. C. Sherriff, *Journey's End* Richard Aldington, *Death of a Hero* Erich Maria Remarque, *All Quiet on the Western Front* Hemingway, *A Farewell to Arms* MacNeice, *Blind Fireworks*	The Wall Street Crash
1930	Masefield becomes Poet Laureate Frederic Manning, *Her Privates We* Auden, *Poems*	
1931	Woolf, *The Waves* Day-Lewis, *From Feathers to Iron*	

Introduction

Hundreds of thousands of poems were written during the First World War and tens of thousands were published during the same period. So voracious was the public's wartime appetite for poetry that, even as early as June 1915, the *Daily Mail* was commenting ruefully that more had 'found its way into print in the last eleven months than in the preceding eleven years'. Yet, despite this extraordinary outpouring of verse and the continuing cultural significance of the Great War, few of these poems are still read today and only a handful of what were called at the time 'soldier poets' are remembered. Siegfried Sassoon and Robert Graves had successful post-war careers, whilst Edward Thomas, Isaac Rosenberg and, to a lesser extent, Ivor Gurney have all been rediscovered by subsequent generations of readers. For most people, however, it is Rupert Brooke and Wilfred Owen who best fulfil the popular image of the war poet. It is their poems which are most frequently anthologised, studied in schools and universities and summoned up in discussion, to the extent that they have almost become required reading for anyone studying the historical, social or cultural impact of the First World War.

Yet this attention is not equally divided between the two. Brooke's name may appear in the contents pages of anthologies and be invoked as frequently as Owen's, but whilst some half a dozen of Owen's poems – 'Strange Meeting', 'Anthem for Doomed Youth', 'Dulce et Decorum est', 'Exposure', 'Spring Offensive', 'Futility' – are consistently reproduced, Brooke's fame as a war poet rests mainly upon 'The Soldier'. Accordingly, it is Owen whose work is more comprehensively discussed and it is Owen who is seen as the more valuable of the two poets. Owen, we are told at great length, was 'the greatest poet of the war', a writer whose ability to combine 'bleak realism with indignation and compassion' enabled him to produce 'some of the finest morally engaged poetry of this century', whilst Brooke is dismissed in a few lines as a naive minor poet whose 'romantic idealism' and 'shining patriotism' epitomise the attitude of a nation ignorant of the slaughter to come. More often than not, Brooke is introduced merely as a foil for Owen or as a way of emphasising the two extremes of the Great War – the idealistic fervour that greeted its outbreak and the horrific reality of the Western Front – and the contrast set up by such approaches, with all their implied notions of value and significance, probably helps to explain why there have been nine separate editions of Owen's poems since his death and only three of Brooke's.

These disparate images of Owen and Brooke are the product of several kinds of selectivity. Representing Brooke's work by using 'The Soldier' or indeed any of the atypical 1914 group of sonnets ignores other more characteristically cynical and witty poems, such as 'A Channel Passage' or 'Lust' from his first book, *Poems*, which was hailed in *The Daily Chronicle* as 'a symptomatic quintessence of the rebellious attitude today' and provoked for him the label of 'an unflinching realist' from *The New Age*. A glance through his later poems reveals the same kind of qualities, suggesting that it is perhaps more instructive to compare 'The Soldier' with 'Heaven' or the sombre and reflective 'Fragment' than with anything by Owen for an accurate assessment of his poetic abilities. Owen, too, has been misrepresented by this kind of selectivity. The emphasis placed upon his more famous war poems refuses to acknowledge the more contemplative response he shows to the war in poems like 'The Send-off' and 'The Calls' or the challenge of the overtly homoerotic 'It was a navy boy' or the sadomasochistic 'The Rime of the Youthful Mariner'. Because he tends to reach his audience through selections – whether overtly in anthology form or covertly in editions of selected poems that nevertheless choose to stress his more bleakly compassionate productions – the sheer breadth and diversity of Owen's oeuvre is rarely remarked upon.

A form of biographical selectivity is also at work here. Both poets' work is all too frequently read in the light of their histories, so that the relationship between life and art becomes binding and the poems are read as a kind of undisguised autobiography. The text, it is implied, becomes a way of assessing the moral qualities or the psychological state of the author, and thus their ethical worth. It is taken for granted, for example, that Brooke's 1914 sonnets were the product of naive jingoistic fervour and that, if he had lived longer and seen more of the realities of war, he would have perhaps produced poems similar to those of Owen or Sassoon. In actual fact, the sonnets were begun after he returned from taking part in the ill-fated Antwerp expedition of October 1914. A letter to Leonard Bacon written shortly afterwards, which describes the event as 'Like Hell, a Dantesque Hell, terrible' and rails against 'half the youth of Europe, blown through pain to nothingness, in the incessant mechanical slaughter of these modern battles', makes it clear that he was not blind to the true nature of the appalling conflict in which he was involved. Similarly, there is a tendency to imply that it was the horrors of war that provoked Owen into writing his most characteristic work. This overlooks the fact that he was still writing and revising such seemingly guileless poems as 'Song of Songs' and 'With an Identity Disc' at Craiglockhart War Hospital after the five-month tour of duty at the Western Front that would furnish him with the raw material for poems like 'The Sentry' and 'The Show'. It was his admiration for Sassoon's work and his subsequent friendship with his idol that shaped his most famous poems, not his initial experiences in the mud of France.

The origins of this selectivity can be traced back to the publication of two books, Brooke's *1914 and Other Poems* (1915) and *Poems by Wilfred Owen* (1920). Both volumes are crucial in establishing their authors' posthumous reputation amongst their contemporaries and both played a vital part in beginning the process of incomplete representation that continues today. In Brooke's case, the process began even before his death, with the enormous popularity of his five wartime sonnets. After his death on 23 April 1915 – symbolically both St George's Day and Shakespeare's birthday – that popularity reached fever pitch, giving rise to the myth of the self-sacrificing warrior aesthete portrayed by Winston Churchill in his obituary of Brooke in *The Times*:

During the last few months of his life, months of preparation in gallant comradeship and open air, the poet-soldier told with all the simple force of genius the sorrow of youth about to die, and the sure and triumphant consolations of a sincere and valiant spirit. He expected to die: he was willing to die for the dear England whose beauty and majesty he knew . . . the thoughts to which he gave expression in the very few incomparable war sonnets which he left behind will be shared by many thousands of young men moving resolutely and blithely foward in this, the hardest, the cruellest, and the least-rewarded of all the wars that men have fought.

Edward Marsh, Brooke's friend since his days at Cambridge, worked quickly to produce a memorial volume and whilst he could not exclude the untypical but famous sonnets, he was careful to also include poems which gave some idea of the full range of Brooke's abilities, from the touching and exotic South Seas poems to the wryly ironic 'The Old Vicarage, Grantchester'. In the event, it was the sonnets that ensured that *1914 and Other Poems* was a bestseller and it was the sonnets, repackaged for an eager public in a separate edition and in anthologies and newspaper reprintings, that came to constitute most readers' idea of Brooke and his poetry. Indeed, so excessive was the rapid mythologising of the 'golden-haired Apollo' and his work that it was seriously proposed that the church clock at Grantchester be permanently fixed at ten to three as a memorial to 'England's noblest son'.

Poems by Wilfred Owen was, in commercial terms at least, much less successful. Despite an enthusiastic reception from reviewers, it failed to sell particularly well and a second, slightly enlarged edition published in 1921 suffered a similar fate. However, it did succeed in its aim of arousing some interest in both Owen's poetry and his personality. Edith Sitwell's selection of poems, carefully made and arranged so as to emphasise Owen's compassion and moral indignation, presented the picture of a tragic, selfless, talented young man whose humanism in the face of wartime atrocity spoke out from every poem. The inclusion of Owen's perplexing Preface, with its stress on 'Poetry' and 'pity', and Sassoon's measured introduction, which spoke of allowing Owen's poems 'backed by the authority of his experience as an infantry soldier' to speak for him, reinforced the picture. Nothing was included that would disrupt this image and it is, to a large extent, Sitwell's and Sassoon's construction of Owen and his work that has survived to this day. It may not have reached a popular audience at the time, but *Poems by Wilfred Owen* laid the foundations for his subsequent recognition – one precursor of which was Arthur Bliss's decision to include 'Spring Offensive' in his *Morning Heroes: A Symphony for Orator, Chorus and Orchestra* (1928).

1928 was also the year in which the Brooke myth first came under serious attack. A decade after the cessation of hostilities, he was still regarded as the epitome of the war poet, aided and abetted by the unspoken agreement amongst ex-combatants that it was, in Osbert Sitwell's words, 'Very bad form / To mention the war' during this period. Then, in 1928, a trickle of novels and autobiographies began to appear – amongst them Sassoon's *Memoirs of a Fox-Hunting Man* – which not only mentioned it, but in the kind of terms that explicitly contradicted the Churchillian view of it as a noble and patriotic adventure. Brooke, of course, was closely associated with this orthodoxy and, as the trickle became a flood over the next two years, strengthened by plays such as R. C. Sherriff's *Journey's End* (1929) and films like Lewis Forman's adaptation of *All Quiet on the Western Front* (1930), it was his poetry that fell out of critical favour. His popular readership remained strong – the new edition of *The Collected Poems of Rupert Brooke: With a Memoir* sold steadily throughout this period – but the arrival of these works which, in the words of a disapproving columnist in *The Times*, were deliberately 'sensational' and showed 'the murky side of war and the bad side of human nature' ensured that he was no longer taken seriously as a war poet by either his fellow-writers or literary critics. His place was taken by Owen, whose reputation was consolidated by the publication of Edmund Blunden's edition of his work in 1931, at the height of what came to be known as 'The War Books Controversy'. It was to Owen, not Brooke, that the new generation of poets such as W. H. Auden and Stephen Spender turned for inspiration and guidance – Cecil Day-Lewis's argument in *A Hope For Poetry* (1934) was that Owen, T. S. Eliot and Gerard Manley Hopkins were the only hope for the future of English poetry – and it is Owen, not Brooke, who is now regarded as the best of the poets to have emerged from 'the war to end all wars'.

GEORGE WALTER

Note on the Text

This Everyman edition reproduces *1914 and Other Poems* and *Poems by Wilfred Owen* side by side for the first time, along with a number of related poems by Brooke and Owen published before the watershed of the late 1920s. Not only does this allow for a greater understanding of the two books that have done so much to shape modern perceptions of Brooke's and Owen's work, but it also provides an insight into the kind of texts encountered by early readers of their poems. In the case of *1914 and Other Poems*, the text is taken from the first impression of June 1915, whilst the text of *Poems by Wilfred Owen* has been taken from the second edition of 1921. The texts of remaining poems have been taken from their first English printing, and the specific sources for these are indicated in the notes that follow the poems. Both Brooke and Owen were planning collections of poetry when they died but, in the event, it was the poems in this edition that became their memorial.

Rupert Brooke

1914 AND OTHER POEMS

1914

I. Peace

Now, God be thanked Who has matched us with His hour,
   And caught our youth, and wakened us from sleeping,
With hand made sure, clear eye, and sharpened power,
   To turn, as swimmers into cleanness leaping,
Glad from a world grown old and cold and weary,   5
   Leave the sick hearts that honour could not move,
And half-men, and their dirty songs and dreary,
   And all the little emptiness of love!

Oh! we, who have known shame, we have found release there,
   Where there's no ill, no grief, but sleep has mending,   10
     Naught broken save this body, lost but breath;
Nothing to shake the laughing heart's long peace there
   But only agony, and that has ending;
     And the worst friend and enemy is but Death.

II. Safety

Dear! of all happy in the hour, most blest
  He who has found our hid security,
Assured in the dark tides of the world that rest,
  And heard our word, 'Who is so safe as we?'
We have found safety with all things undying,   5
  The winds, and morning, tears of men and mirth,
The deep night, and birds singing, and clouds flying,
  And sleep, and freedom, and the autumnal earth.
We have built a house that is not for Time's throwing.
  We have gained a peace unshaken by pain for ever.   10
War knows no power. Safe shall be my going,
  Secretly armed against all death's endeavour;
Safe though all safety's lost; safe where men fall;
And if these poor limbs die, safest of all.

III. The Dead

Blow out, you bugles, over the rich Dead!
   There's none of these so lonely and poor of old,
   But, dying, has made us rarer gifts than gold.
These laid the world away; poured out the red
Sweet wine of youth; gave up the years to be   5
   Of work and joy, and that unhoped serene,
   That men call age; and those who would have been,
Their sons, they gave, their immortality.

Blow, bugles, blow! They brought us, for our dearth,
   Holiness, lacked so long, and Love, and Pain.   10
Honour has come back, as a king, to earth,
   And paid his subjects with a royal wage;
And Nobleness walks in our ways again;
   And we have come into our heritage.

IV. The Dead

These hearts were woven of human joys and cares,
    Washed marvellously with sorrow, swift to mirth.
The years had given them kindness. Dawn was theirs,
    And sunset, and the colours of the earth.
These had seen movement, and heard music; known   5
    Slumber and waking; loved; gone proudly friended;
Felt the quick stir of wonder; sat alone;
    Touched flowers and furs and cheeks. All this is ended.

There are waters blown by changing winds to laughter
And lit by the rich skies, all day. And after,   10
    Frost, with a gesture, stays the waves that dance
And wandering loveliness. He leaves a white
    Unbroken glory, a gathered radiance,
A width, a shining peace, under the night.

V. The Soldier

If I should die, think only this of me:
  That there's some corner of a foreign field
That is for ever England. There shall be
  In that rich earth a richer dust concealed;
A dust whom England bore, shaped, made aware,   5
  Gave, once, her flowers to love, her ways to roam,
A body of England's, breathing English air,
  Washed by the rivers, blest by suns of home.

And think, this heart, all evil shed away,
  A pulse in the eternal mind, no less   10
    Gives somewhere back the thoughts by England given;
Her sights and sounds; dreams happy as her day;
  And laughter, learnt of friends; and gentleness,
    In hearts at peace, under an English heaven.

The Treasure

When colour goes home into the eyes,
   And lights that shine are shut again
With dancing girls and sweet birds' cries
   Behind the gateways of the brain;
And that no-place which gave them birth, shall close   5
The rainbow and the rose:–

Still may Time hold some golden space
   Where I'll unpack that scented store
Of song and flower and sky and face,
   And count, and touch, and turn them o'er,   10
Musing upon them; as a mother, who
Has watched her children all the rich day through,
Sits, quiet-handed, in the fading light,
When children sleep, ere night.

The South Seas

Tiare Tahiti

Mamua, when our laughter ends,
And hearts and bodies, brown as white,
Are dust about the doors of friends,
Or scent ablowing down the night,
Then, oh! then, the wise agree,   5
Comes our immortality.
Mamua, there waits a land
Hard for us to understand.
Out of time, beyond the sun,
All are one in Paradise,   10
You and Pupure are one,
And Taü, and the ungainly wise.
There the Eternals are, and there
The Good, the Lovely, and the True,
And Types, whose earthly copies were   15
The foolish broken things we knew;
There is the Face, whose ghosts we are;
The real, the never-setting Star;
And the Flower, of which we love
Faint and fading shadows here;
Never a tear, but only Grief;   20
Dance, but not the limbs that move;
Songs in Song shall disappear;
Instead of lovers, Love shall be;
For hearts, Immutability;
And there, on the Ideal Reef,   25
Thunders the Everlasting Sea!

    And my laughter, and my pain,
Shall home to the Eternal Brain.
And all lovely things, they say,
Meet in Loveliness again;   30
Miri's laugh, Teïpo's feet,

And the hands of Matua,
Stars and sunlight there shall meet
Coral's hues and rainbows there,
And Teüra's braided hair;   35
And with the starred *tiare's* white,
And white birds in the dark ravine,
And *flamboyants* ablaze at night,
And jewels, and evening's after-green,
And dawns of pearl and gold and red,   40
Mamua, your lovelier head!
And there'll no more be one who dreams
Under the ferns, of crumbling stuff,
Eyes of illusion, mouth that seems,
All time-entangled human love.   45
And you'll no longer swing and sway
Divinely down the scented shade,
Where feet to Ambulation fade,
And moons are lost in endless Day.
How shall we wind these wreaths of ours,   50
Where there are neither heads nor flowers?
Oh, Heaven's Heaven! – but we'll be missing
The palms, and sunlight, and the south;
And there's an end, I think, of kissing,
When our mouths are one with Mouth. . . .   55

    Taü here, Mamua,
Crown the hair, and come away!
Hear the calling of the moon,
And the whispering scents that stray
About the idle warm lagoon.   60
Hasten, hand in human hand,
Down the dark, the flowered way,
Along the whiteness of the sand,
And in the water's soft caress,
Wash the mind of foolishness,   65
Mamua, until the day.
Spend the glittering moonlight there
Pursuing down the soundless deep
Limbs that gleam and shadowy hair,
Or floating lazy, half-asleep.   70

Dive and double and follow after,
Snare in flowers, and kiss, and call,
With lips that fade, and human laughter
And faces individual,
Well this side of Paradise! . . .   75
    There's little comfort in the wise.

                    Papeete, February 1914

Retrospect

In your arms was still delight,
Quiet as a street at night;
And thoughts of you, I do remember,
Were green leaves in a darkened chamber,
Were dark clouds in a moonless sky.   5
Love, in you, went passing by,
Penetrative, remote, and rare,
Like a bird in the wide air,
And, as the bird, it left no trace
In the heaven of your face.   10
In your stupidity I found
The sweet hush after a sweet sound.
All about you was the light
That dims the greying end of night;
Desire was the unrisen sun,   15
Joy the day not yet begun,
With tree whispering to tree,
Without wind, quietly.
Wisdom slept within your hair,
And Long-Suffering was there,   20
And, in the flowing of your dress,
Undiscerning Tenderness.
And when you thought, it seemed to me,
Infinitely, and like a sea,
About the slight world you had known   25
Your vast unconsciousness was thrown. . . .

    O haven without wave or tide!
Silence, in which all songs have died!
Holy book, where hearts are still!
And home at length under the hill!   30
O mother quiet, breasts of peace,
Where love itself would faint and cease!
O infinite deep I never knew,
I would come back, come back to you,

Find you, as a pool unstirred,   35
Kneel down by you, and never a word,
Lay my head, and nothing said,
In your hands, ungarlanded;
And a long watch you would keep;
And I should sleep, and I should sleep!   40

Mataiea, January 1914

The Great Lover

I have been so great a lover: filled my days
So proudly with the splendour of Love's praise,
The pain, the calm, and the astonishment,
Desire illimitable, and still content,
And all dear names men use, to cheat despair,   5
For the perplexed and viewless streams that bear
Our hearts at random down the dark of life.
Now, ere the unthinking silence on that strife
Steals down, I would cheat drowsy Death so far,
My night shall be remembered for a star   10
That outshone all the suns of all men's days.
Shall I not crown them with immortal praise
Whom I have loved, who have given me, dared with me
High secrets, and in darkness knelt to see
The inenarrable godhead of delight?   15
Love is a flame; – we have beaconed the world's night.
A city: – and we have built it, these and I.
An emperor: – we have taught the world to die.
So, for their sakes I loved, ere I go hence,
And the high cause of Love's magnificence,   20
And to keep loyalties young, I'll write those names
Golden for ever, eagles, crying flames,
And set them as a banner, that men may know,
To dare the generations, burn, and blow
Out on the wind of Time, shining and streaming. . . .   25

These I have loved:
                        White plates and cups, clean-gleaming,
Ringed with blue lines; and feathery, faery dust;
Wet roofs, beneath the lamp-light; the strong crust
Of friendly bread; and many-tasting food;
Rainbows; and the blue bitter smoke of wood;   30
And radiant raindrops couching in cool flowers;
And flowers themselves, that sway through sunny hours,
Dreaming of moths that drink them under the moon;

Then, the cool kindliness of sheets, that soon
Smooth away trouble; and the rough male kiss   35
Of blankets; grainy wood; live hair that is
Shining and free; blue-massing clouds; the keen
Unpassioned beauty of a great machine;
The benison of hot water; furs to touch;
The good smell of old clothes; and other such –   40
The comfortable smell of friendly fingers,
Hair's fragrance, and the musty reek that lingers
About dead leaves and last year's ferns. . . .
         Dear names,
And thousand other throng to me! Royal flames;
Sweet water's dimpling laugh from tap or spring;   45
Holes in the ground; and voices that do sing;
Voices in laughter, too; and body's pain,
Soon turned to peace; and the deep-panting train;
Firm sands; the little dulling edge of foam
That browns and dwindles as the wave goes home;   50
And washen stones, gay for an hour; the cold
Graveness of iron; moist black earthen mould;
Sleep; and high places; footprints in the dew;
And oaks; and brown horse-chestnuts, glossy-new;
And new-peeled sticks; and shining pools on grass; –   55
All these have been my loves. And these shall pass,
Whatever passes not, in the great hour,
Nor all my passion, all my prayers, have power
To hold them with me through the gate of Death.
They'll play deserter, turn with the traitor breath,   60
Break the high bond we made, and sell Love's trust
And sacramented covenant to the dust.
—Oh, never a doubt but, somewhere, I shall wake,
And give what's left of love again, and make
New friends, now strangers. . . .
        But the best I've known,   65
Stays here, and changes, breaks, grows old, is blown
About the winds of the world, and fades from brains
Of living men, and dies.
       Nothing remains.

O dear my loves, O faithless, once again

This one last gift I give: that after men   70
Shall know, and later lovers, far-removed,
Praise you, 'All these were lovely'; say, 'He loved.'

Mataiea, 1914

Heaven

Fish (fly-replete, in depth of June,
Dawdling away their wat'ry noon)
Ponder deep wisdom, dark or clear,
Each secret fishy hope or fear.
Fish say, they have their Stream and Pond;   5
But is there anything Beyond?
This life cannot be All, they swear,
For how unpleasant, if it were!
One may not doubt that, somehow, Good
Shall come of Water and of Mud;   10
And, sure, the reverent eye must see
A Purpose in Liquidity.
We darkly know, by Faith we cry,
The future is not Wholly Dry.
Mud unto mud! – Death eddies near –   15
Not here the appointed End, not here!
But somewhere, beyond Space and Time,
Is wetter water, slimier slime!
And there (they trust) there swimmeth One
Who swam ere rivers were begun,   20
Immense, of fishy form and mind,
Squamous, omnipotent, and kind;
And under that Almighty Fin,
The littlest fish may enter in.
Oh! never fly conceals a hook,   25
Fish say, in the Eternal Brook,
But more than mundane weeds are there,
And mud, celestially fair;
Fat caterpillars drift around,
And Paradisal grubs are found;   30
Unfading moths, immortal flies,
And the worm that never dies.
And in that Heaven of all their wish,
There shall be no more land, say fish.

Doubts

When she sleeps, her soul, I know,
Goes a wanderer on the air,
Wings where I may never go,
Leaves her lying, still and fair,
Waiting, empty, laid aside,   5
Like a dress upon a chair. . . .
This I know, and yet I know
Doubts that will not be denied.

For if the soul be not in place,
What has laid trouble in her face?   10
And, sits there nothing ware and wise
Behind the curtains of her eyes,
What is it, in the self's eclipse,
Shadows, soft and passingly,
About the corners of her lips,   15
The smile that is essential she?

And if the spirit be not there,
Why is fragrance in the hair?

There's Wisdom in Women

'Oh love is fair, and love is rare;' my dear one she said,
'But love goes lightly over.' I bowed her foolish head,
And kissed her hair and laughed at her. Such a child was she;
So new to love, so true to love, and she spoke so bitterly.

But there's wisdom in women, of more than they have
    known,   5
And thoughts go blowing through them, are wiser than their
    own,
Or how should my dear one, being ignorant and young,
Have cried on love so bitterly, with so true a tongue?

He wonders whether to praise or to blame her

I have peace to weigh your worth, now all is over,
   But if to praise or blame you, cannot say.
For who decries the loved, decries the lover;
   Yet what man lauds the thing he's thrown away?

Be you, in truth, this dull, slight, cloudy naught,   5
   The more fool I, so great a fool to adore;
But if you're that high goddess once I thought,
   The more your godhead is, I lose the more.

Dear fool, pity the fool who thought you clever!
   Dear wisdom, do not mock the fool that missed you!   10
Most fair, – the blind has lost your face for ever!
   Most foul, – how could I see you while I kissed you?

So . . . the poor love of fools and blind I've proved you,
For, foul or lovely, 'twas a fool that loved you.

A Memory

(From a sonnet-sequence)

Somewhile before the dawn I rose, and stept
   Softly along the dim way to your room,
   And found you sleeping in the quiet gloom,
And holiness about you as you slept.
I knelt there; till your waking fingers crept   5
   About my head, and held it. I had rest
   Unhoped this side of Heaven, beneath your breast.
I knelt a long time, still; nor even wept.

It was great wrong you did me; and for gain
Of that poor moment's kindliness, and ease,   10
And sleepy mother-comfort!
                  Child, you know
How easily love leaps out to dreams like these,
Who has seen them true. And love that's wakened so
Takes all too long to lay asleep again.

                        Waikiki, October 1913

One Day

Today I have been happy. All the day
   I held the memory of you, and wove
Its laughter with the dancing light o' the spray,
   And sowed the sky with tiny clouds of love,
And sent you following the white waves of sea,   5
   And crowned your head with fancies, nothing worth,
Stray buds from that old dust of misery,
   Being glad with a new foolish quiet mirth.

So lightly I played with those dark memories,
Just as a child, beneath the summer skies,   10
   Plays hour by hour with a strange shining stone,
For which (he knows not) towns were fire of old,
   And love has been betrayed, and murder done,
And great kings turned to a little bitter mould.

               The Pacific, October 1913

Waikiki

Warm perfumes like a breath from vine and tree
   Drift down the darkness. Plangent, hidden from eyes,
   Somewhere an *eukaleli* thrills and cries
And stabs with pain the night's brown savagery.
And dark scents whisper; and dim waves creep to me,   5
   Gleam like a woman's hair, stretch out, and rise;
   And new stars burn into the ancient skies,
Over the murmurous soft Hawaian sea.

And I recall, lose, grasp, forget again,
   And still remember, a tale I have heard, or known   10
An empty tale, of idleness and pain,
   Of two that loved – or did not love – and one
Whose perplexed heart did evil, foolishly,
A long while since, and by some other sea.

Waikiki, 1913

Hauntings

In the grey tumult of these after years
   Oft silence falls; the incessant wranglers part;
And less-than-echoes of remembered tears
   Hush all the loud confusion of the heart;
And a shade, through the toss'd ranks of mirth and crying   5
   Hungers, and pains, and each dull passionate mood, –
Quite lost, and all but all forgot, undying,
   Comes back the ecstasy of your quietude.

So a poor ghost, beside his misty streams,
Is haunted by strange doubts, evasive dreams,   10
   Hints of a pre-Lethean life, of men,
Stars, rocks, and flesh, things unintelligible,
   And light on waving grass, he knows not when,
And feet that ran, but where, he cannot tell.

The Pacific, 1914

Sonnet

(Suggested by some of the Proceedings
of the Society for Psychical Research)

Not with vain tears, when we're beyond the sun,
　We'll beat on the substantial doors, nor tread
　Those dusty high-roads of the aimless dead
Plaintive for Earth; but rather turn and run
Down some close-covered by-way of the air,　　　　　5
　Some low sweet alley between wind and wind,
　Stoop under faint gleams, thread the shadows, find
Some whispering ghost-forgotten nook, and there

Spend in pure converse our eternal day;
　Think each in each, immediately wise;　　　　　10
Learn all we lacked before; hear, know, and say
　What this tumultuous body now denies;
And feel, who have laid our groping hands away;
　And see, no longer blinded by our eyes.

Clouds

Down the blue night the unending columns press
   In noiseless tumult, break and wave and flow,
   Now tread the far South, or lift rounds of snow
Up to the white moon's hidden loveliness.
Some pause in their grave wandering comradeless,   5
   And turn with profound gesture vague and slow,
   As who would pray good for the world, but know
Their benediction empty as they bless.

They say that the Dead die not, but remain
   Near to the rich heirs of their grief and mirth.   10
      I think they ride the calm mid-heaven, as these,
In wise majestic melancholy train,
   And watch the moon, and the still-raging seas,
And men, coming and going on the earth.

                                   The Pacific, October 1913

Mutability

They say there's a high windless world and strange,
　　Out of the wash of days and temporal tide,
　　Where Faith and Good, Wisdom and Truth abide,
Æterna corpora, subject to no change.
There the sure suns of these pale shadows move;　　　　　　5
　　There stand the immortal ensigns of our war;
　　Our melting flesh fixed Beauty there, a star,
And perishing hearts, imperishable Love. . . .

Dear, we know only that we sigh, kiss, smile;
　　Each kiss lasts but the kissing; and grief goes over;　　　10
　　Love has no habitation but the heart.
Poor straws! on the dark flood we catch awhile,
　　Cling, and are borne into the night apart.
　　The laugh dies with the lips, 'Love' with the lover.

South Kensington – Makaweli, 1913

Other Poems

The Busy Heart

Now that we've done our best and worst, and parted,
 I would fill my mind with thoughts that will not rend.
(O heart, I do not dare go empty-hearted)
 I'll think of Love in books, Love without end;
Women with child, content; and old men sleeping;   5
 And wet strong ploughlands, scarred for certain grain;
And babes that weep, and so forget their weeping;
 And the young heavens, forgetful after rain;
And evening hush, broken by homing wings;
 And Song's nobility, and Wisdom holy,   10
That live, we dead. I would think of a thousand things,
 Lovely and durable, and taste them slowly,
One after one, like tasting a sweet food.
I have need to busy my heart with quietude.

Love

Love is a breach in the walls, a broken gate,
    Where that comes in that shall not go again;
Love sells the proud heart's citadel to Fate.
    They have known shame, who love unloved. Even then
When two mouths, thirsty each for each, find slaking,   5
    And agony's forgot, and hushed the crying
Of credulous hearts, in heaven – such are but taking
    Their own poor dreams within their arms, and lying
Each in his lonely night, each with a ghost.
    Some share that night. But they know, love grows colder,   10
Grows false and dull, that was sweet lies at most.
    Astonishment is no more in hand or shoulder,
But darkens, and dies out from kiss to kiss.
All this is love; and all love is but this.

Unfortunate

Heart, you are restless as a paper scrap
   That's tossed down dusty pavements by the wind;
   Saying, 'She is most wise, patient and kind.
Between the small hands folded in her lap
Surely a shamed head may bow down at length,   5
   And find forgiveness where the shadows stir
About her lips, and wisdom in her strength,
   Peace in her peace. Come to her, come to her!' . . .

She will not care. She'll smile to see me come,
   So that I think all Heaven in flower to fold me.   10
   She'll give me all I ask, kiss me and hold me,
      And open wide upon that holy air
The gates of peace, and take my tiredness home,
      Kinder than God. But, heart, she will not care.

The Chilterns

Your hands, my dear, adorable,
　　Your lips of tenderness
– Oh, I've loved you faithfully and well,
　　Three years, or a bit less.
　　It wasn't a success.　　　　　　　　　　　　　5

Thank God, that's done! and I'll take the road,
　　Quit of my youth and you,
The Roman road to Wendover
　　By Tring and Lilley Hoo,
　　As a free man may do.　　　　　　　　　　　10

For youth goes over, the joys that fly,
　　The tears that follow fast;
And the dirtiest things we do must lie
　　Forgotten at the last;
　　Even Love goes past.　　　　　　　　　　　15

What's left behind I shall not find,
　　The splendour and the pain;
The splash of sun, the shouting wind,
　　And the brave sting of rain,
　　I may not meet again.　　　　　　　　　　　20

But the years, that take the best away,
　　Give something in the end;
And a better friend than love have they,
　　For none to mar or mend,
　　That have themselves to friend.　　　　　　25

I shall desire and I shall find
　　The best of my desires;
The autumn road, the mellow wind
　　That soothes the darkening shires,
　　And laughter, and inn-fires.　　　　　　　　30

White mist about the black hedgerows,
  The slumbering Midland plain,
The silence where the clover grows,
  And the dead leaves in the lane,
  Certainly, these remain. 35

And I shall find some girl perhaps,
  And a better one than you,
With eyes as wise, but kindlier,
  And lips as soft, but true.
  And I daresay she will do. 40

Home

I came back late and tired last night
  Into my little room,
To the long chair and the firelight
  And comfortable gloom.

But as I entered softly in   5
  I saw a woman there,
The line of neck and cheek and chin,
  The darkness of her hair,
The form of one I did not know
  Sitting in my chair.   10

I stood a moment fierce and still,
  Watching her neck and hair.
I made a step to her; and saw
  That there was no one there.

It was some trick of the firelight   15
  That made me see her there.
It was a chance of shade and light
  And the cushion in the chair.

Oh, all you happy over the earth,
  That night, how could I sleep?   20
I lay and watched the lonely gloom;
  And watched the moonlight creep
From wall to basin, round the room.
  All night I could not sleep.

The Night Journey

Hands and lit faces eddy to a line;
   The dazed last minutes click; the clamour dies.
Beyond the great-swung arc o' the roof, divine,
   Night, smoky-scarv'd, with thousand coloured eyes

Glares the imperious mystery of the way.   5
   Thirsty for dark, you feel the long-limbed train
Throb, stretch, thrill motion, slide, pull out and sway,
   Strain for the far, pause, draw to strength again. . . .

As a man, caught by some great hour, will rise,
   Slow-limbed, to meet the light or find his love;   10
And, breathing long, with staring sightless eyes,
   Hands out, head back, agape and silent, move

Sure as a flood, smooth as a vast wind blowing;
   And, gathering power and purpose as he goes,
Unstumbling, unreluctant, strong, unknowing,   15
   Borne by a will not his, that lifts, that grows,

Sweep out to darkness, triumphing in his goal,
   Out of the fire, out of the little room. . . .
– There is an end appointed, O my soul!
   Crimson and green the signals burn; the gloom   20

Is hung with steam's far-blowing livid streamers.
   Lost into God, as lights in light, we fly,
Grown one with will, end-drunken huddled dreamers.
   The white lights roar. The sounds of the world die.

And lips and laughter are forgotten things.   25
   Speed sharpens; grows. Into the night, and on,
The strength and splendour of our purpose swings.
   The lamps fade; and the stars. We are alone.

Song

All suddenly the wind comes soft,
   And Spring is here again;
And the hawthorn quickens with buds of green,
   And my heart with buds of pain.

My heart all Winter lay so numb,   5
   The earth so dead and frore,
That I never thought the Spring would come,
   Or my heart wake any more.

But Winter's broken and earth has woken,
   And the small birds cry again;   10
And the hawthorn hedge puts forth its buds,
   And my heart puts forth its pain.

Beauty and Beauty

When Beauty and Beauty meet
   All naked, fair to fair,
The earth is crying-sweet,
   And scattering-bright the air,
Eddying, dizzying, closing round,   5
   With soft and drunken laughter;
Veiling all that may befall
   After – after –

Where Beauty and Beauty met,
   Earth's still a-tremble there,   10
And winds are scented yet,
   And memory-soft the air,
Bosoming, folding glints of light,
   And shreds of shadowy laughter;
Not the tears that fill the years   15
   After– after –

The Way that Lovers use

The way that lovers use is this;
  They bow, catch hands, with never a word,
And their lips meet, and they do kiss,
  – So I have heard.

They queerly find some healing so,   5
  And strange attainment in the touch;
There is a secret lovers know,
  – I have read as much.

And theirs no longer joy nor smart,
  Changing or ending, night or day;   10
But mouth to mouth, and heart on heart,
  – So lovers say.

Mary and Gabriel

Young Mary, loitering once her garden way,
Felt a warm splendour grow in the April day,
As wine that blushes water through. And soon,
Out of the gold air of the afternoon,
One knelt before her: hair he had, or fire,   5
Bound back above his ears with golden wire,
Baring the eager marble of his face.
Not man's nor woman's was the immortal grace
Rounding the limbs beneath that robe of white,
And lighting the proud eyes with changeless light,   10
Incurious. Calm as his wings, and fair,
That presence filled the garden.
                                        She stood there,
Saying, 'What would you, Sir?'
                                        He told his word,
'Blessed art thou of women!' Half she heard,
Hands folded and face bowed, half long had known,   15
The message of that clear and holy tone,
That fluttered hot sweet sobs about her heart;
Such serene tidings moved such human smart.
Her breath came quick as little flakes of snow.
Her hands crept up her breast. She did but know   20
It was not hers. She felt a trembling stir
Within her body, a will too strong for her
That held and filled and mastered all. With eyes
Closed, and a thousand soft short broken sighs,
She gave submission; fearful, meek, and glad. . . .   25

She wished to speak. Under her breasts she had
Such multitudinous burnings, to and fro,
And throbs not understood; she did not know
If they were hurt or joy for her; but only
That she was grown strange to herself, half lonely,   30
All wonderful, filled full of pains to come
And thoughts she dare not think, swift thoughts and dumb,

Human, and quaint, her own, yet very far,
Divine, dear, terrible, familiar . . .
Her heart was faint for telling; to relate   35
Her limbs' sweet treachery, her strange high estate,
Over and over, whispering, half revealing,
Weeping; and so find kindness to her healing.
'Twixt tears and laughter, panic hurrying her,
She raised her eyes to that fair messenger.   40
He knelt unmoved, immortal; with his eyes
Gazing beyond her, calm to the calm skies;
Radiant, untroubled in his wisdom, kind.
His sheaf of lilies stirred not in the wind.
How should she, pitiful with mortality,   45
Try the wide peace of that felicity
With ripples of her perplexed shaken heart,
And hints of human ecstasy, human smart,
And whispers of the lonely weight she bore,
And how her womb within was hers no more   50
And at length hers?
                        Being tired, she bowed her head;
And said, 'So be it!'
                        The great wings were spread,
Showering glory on the fields, and fire.
The whole air, singing, bore him up, and higher,
Unswerving, unreluctant. Soon he shone   55
A gold speck in the gold skies; then was gone.

The air was colder, and grey. She stood alone.

The Funeral of Youth: Threnody

The day that *Youth* had died,
There came to his grave-side,
In decent mourning, from the country's ends,
Those scatter'd friends
Who had lived the boon companions of his prime,   5
And laughed with him and sung with him and wasted,
In feast and wine and many-crown'd carouse,
The days and nights and dawnings of the time
When *Youth* kept open house,
Nor left untasted   10
Aught of his high emprise and ventures dear,
No quest of his unshar'd –
All these, with loitering feet and sad head bar'd,
Followed their old friend's bier.
Folly went first,   15
With muffled bells and coxcomb still revers'd;
And after trod the bearers, hat in hand –
Laughter, most hoarse, and Captain *Pride* with tanned
And martial face all grim, and fussy *Joy*,
Who had to catch a train, and *Lust*, poor, snivelling boy;   20
These bore the dear departed.
Behind them, broken-hearted,
Came *Grief*, so noisy a widow, that all said,
'Had he but wed
Her elder sister *Sorrow*, in her stead!'
And by her, trying to soothe her all the time,
The fatherless children, *Colour*, *Tune*, and *Rhyme*
(The sweed lad *Rhyme*), ran all-uncomprehending.
Then, at the way's sad ending,
Round the raw grave they stay'd. Old *Wisdom* read,   30
In mumbling tone, the Service for the Dead.
There stood *Romance*,
The furrowing tears had mark'd her rougèd cheek;
Poor old *Conceit*, his wonder unassuaged;
Dead *Innocency's* daughter, *Ignorance*;   35

And shabby, ill-dress'd *Generosity*;
And *Argument*, too full of woe to speak;
Passion, grown portly, something middle-aged;
And *Friendship* – not a minute older, she;
Impatience, ever taking out his watch;   40
Faith, who was deaf, and had to lean, to catch
Old *Wisdom's* endless drone.
Beauty was there,
Pale in her black; dry-eyed; she stood alone.
Poor maz'd *Imagination*; *Fancy* wild;   45
Ardour, the sunlight on his greying hair;
Contentment, who had known *Youth* as a child
And never seen him since. And *Spring* came too,
Dancing over the tombs, and brought him flowers –
She did not stay for long.   50
And *Truth*, and *Grace*, and all the merry crew,
The laughing *Winds* and *Rivers*, and lithe *Hours*;
And *Hope*, the dewy-eyed; and sorrowing *Song*;–
Yes, with much woe and mourning general,
At dead *Youth's* funeral,   55
Even these were met once more together, all,
Who erst the fair and living *Youth* did know;
All, except only *Love*. *Love* had died long ago.

Grantchester

The Old Vicarage, Grantchester

(Café des Westens, Berlin, May 1912)

Just now the lilac is in bloom,
All before my little room;
And in my flower-beds, I think,
Smile the carnation and the pink;
And down the borders, well I know,   5
The poppy and the pansy blow . . .
Oh! there the chestnuts, summer through,
Beside the river make for you
A tunnel of green gloom, and sleep
Deeply above; and green and deep   10
The stream mysterious glides beneath,
Green as a dream and deep as death.
– Oh, damn! I know it! and I know
How the May fields all golden show,
And when the day is young and sweet,   15
Gild gloriously the bare feet
That run to bathe . . .
                    Du lieber Gott!

Here am I, sweating, sick, and hot,
And there the shadowed waters fresh
Lean up to embrace the naked flesh.   20
Temperamentvoll German Jews
Drink beer around; – and *there* the dews
Are soft beneath a morn of gold.
Here tulips bloom as they are told;
Unkempt about those hedges blows   25
An English unofficial rose;
And there the unregulated sun
Slopes down to rest when day is done,

And wakes a vague unpunctual star,
A slippered Hesper; and there are   30
Meads towards Haslingfield and Coton
Where *das Betreten*'s not *verboten*.

εἴθε γενοίμην . . . would I were
In Grantchester, in Grantchester! –
Some, it may be, can get in touch   35
With Nature there, or Earth, or such.
And clever modern men have seen
A Faun a-peeping through the green,
And felt the Classics were not dead,
To glimpse a Naiad's reedy head,   40
Or hear the Goat-foot piping low: . . .
But these are things I do not know.
I only know that you may lie
Day long and watch the Cambridge sky,
And, flower-lulled in sleepy grass,   45
Hear the cool lapse of hours pass,
Until the centuries blend and blur
In Grantchester, in Grantchester. . . .
Still in the dawnlit waters cool
His ghostly Lordship swims his pool,   50
And tries the strokes, essays the tricks,
Long learnt on Hellespont, or Styx.
Dan Chaucer hears his river still
Chatter beneath a phantom mill.
Tennyson notes, with studious eye,   55
How Cambridge waters hurry by . . .
And in that garden, black and white,
Creep whispers through the grass all night;
And spectral dance, before the dawn,
A hundred Vicars down the lawn;   60
Curates, long dust, will come and go
On lissom, clerical, printless toe;
And oft between the boughs is seen
The sly shade of a Rural Dean . . .
Till, at a shiver in the skies,   65
Vanishing with Satanic cries,
The prim ecclesiastic rout

Leaves but a startled sleeper-out,
Grey heavens, the first bird's drowsy calls,
The falling house that never falls.   70

God! I will pack, and take a train,
And get me to England once again!
For England's the one land, I know,
Where men with Splendid Hearts may go;
And Cambridgeshire, of all England,   75
The shire for Men who Understand;
And of *that* district I prefer
The lovely hamlet Grantchester.
For Cambridge people rarely smile,
Being urban, squat, and packed with guile;   80
And Royston men in the far South
Are black and fierce and strange of mouth;
At Over they fling oaths at one,
And worse than oaths at Trumpington,
And Ditton girls are mean and dirty,   85
And there's none in Harston under thirty,
And folks in Shelford and those parts
Have twisted lips and twisted hearts,
And Barton men make Cockney rhymes,
And Coton's full of nameless crimes,   90
And things are done you'd not believe
At Madingley, on Christmas Eve.
Strong men have run for miles and miles,
When one from Cherry Hinton smiles;
Strong men have blanched, and shot their wives,   95
Rather than send them to St Ives;
Strong men have cried like babes, bydam,
To hear what happened at Babraham.
But Grantchester! ah, Grantchester!
There's peace and holy quiet there,   100
Great clouds along pacific skies,
And men and women with straight eyes,
Lithe children lovelier than a dream,
A bosky wood, a slumbrous stream,
And little kindly winds that creep   105
Round twilight corners, half asleep.

In Grantchester their skins are white;
They bathe by day, they bathe by night;
The women there do all they ought;
The men observe the Rules of Thought.   110
They love the Good; they worship Truth;
They laugh uproariously in youth;
(And when they get to feeling old,
They up and shoot themselves, I'm told) . . .

Ah God! to see the branches stir   115
Across the moon at Grantchester!
To smell the thrilling-sweet and rotten
Unforgettable, unforgotten
River-smell, and hear the breeze
Sobbing in the little trees.   120
Say, do the elm-clumps greatly stand
Still guardians of that holy land?
The chestnuts shade, in reverend dream,
The yet unacademic stream?
Is dawn a secret shy and cold   125
Anadyomene, silver-gold?
And sunset still a golden sea
From Haslingfield to Madingley?
And after, ere the night is born,
Do hares come out about the corn?   130
Oh, is the water sweet and cool,
Gentle and brown, above the pool?
And laughs the immortal river still
Under the mill, under the mill?
Say, is there Beauty yet to find?   135
And Certainty? and Quiet kind?
Deep meadows yet, for to forget
The lies, and truths, and pain? . . . oh! yet
Stands the Church clock at ten to three?
And is there honey still for tea?   140

Other Related Poems

Fafaïa

Stars that seem so close and bright,
Watched by lovers through the night,
Swim in emptiness, men say,
Many a mile and year away.

And yonder star that burns so white,   5
May have died to dust and night
Ten, maybe, or fifteen year,
Before it shines upon my dear.

Oh! often among men below,
Heart cries out to heart, I know,   10
And one is dust a many years,
Child, before the other hears.

Heart from heart is all as far,
Fafaïa, as star from star.

Saanapu, November 1913

A Song

As the Wind, and as the Wind,
   In a corner of the way,
Goes stepping, stands twirling,
Invisibly, comes whirling,
Bows before, and skips behind,   5
   In a grave, an endless play –

So my Heart, and so my Heart,
   Following where your feet have gone,
Stirs dust of old dreams there;
He turns a toe; he gleams there,   10
Treading you a dance apart.
   But you see not. You pass on.

April 1915

Fragment

I strayed about the deck, an hour, tonight
Under a cloudy moonless sky; and peeped
In at the windows, watched my friends at table,
Or playing cards, or standing in the doorway,
Or coming out into the darkness. Still   5
No one could see me.

                 I would have thought of them
– Heedless, within a week of battle – in pity,
Pride in their strength and in the weight and firmness
And link'd beauty of bodies, and pity that
This gay machine of splendour 'ld soon be broken,   10
Thought little of, pashed, scattered. . . .

                     Only, always,
I could but see them – against the lamplight – pass
Like coloured shadows, thinner than filmy glass,
Slight bubbles, fainter than the wave's faint light,
That broke to phosphorus out in the night,   15
Perishing things and strange ghosts – soon to die
To other ghosts – this one, or that, or I.

                          April 1915

Wilfred Owen

Poems by Wilfred Owen

Preface

This book is not about heroes. English Poetry is not yet fit to speak of them. Nor is it about deeds or lands, nor anything about glory, honour, dominion or power,

except War.

Above all, this book is not concerned with Poetry.
The subject of it is War, and the pity of War.
The Poetry is in the pity.
Yet these elegies are not to this generation,
     This is in no sense consolatory.

They may be to the next.
All the poet can do today is to warn.
That is why the true Poets must be truthful.
If I thought the letter of this book would last,
I might have used proper names; but if the spirit of it survives Prussia, – my ambition and those names will be content; for they will have achieved themselves fresher fields than Flanders.

(Note – This Preface was found, in an unfinished condition, among Wilfred Owen's papers.)

Strange Meeting

It seemed that out of the battle I escaped
Down some profound dull tunnel, long since scooped
Through granites which Titanic wars had groined.
Yet also there encumbered sleepers groaned,
Too fast in thought or death to be bestirred.   5
Then, as I probed them, one sprang up, and stared
With piteous recognition in fixed eyes,
Lifting distressful hands as if to bless.
And by his smile, I knew that sullen hall;
With a thousand fears that vision's face was grained;   10
Yet no blood reached there from the upper ground,
And no guns thumped, or down the flues made moan.
'Strange, friend,' I said, 'Here is no cause to mourn.'
'None,' said the other, 'Save the undone years,
The hopelessness Whatever hope is yours,   15
Was my life also; I went hunting wild
After the wildest beauty in the world,
Which lies not calm in eyes, or braided hair,
But mocks the steady running of the hour,
And if it grieves, grieves richlier than here.   20
For by my glee might many men have laughed,
And of my weeping something has been left,
Which must die now. I mean the truth untold,
The pity of war, the pity war distilled.
Now men will go content with what we spoiled.   25
Or, discontent, boil bloody, and be spilled.
They will be swift with swiftness of the tigress,
None will break ranks, though nations trek from progress.
Courage was mine, and I had mystery;
Wisdom was mine, and I had mastery;   30
To miss the march of this retreating world
Into vain citadels that are not walled.
Then, when much blood had clogged their chariot-wheels
I would go up and wash them from sweet wells,
Even with truths that lie too deep for taint.   35

I would have poured my spirit without stint
But not through wounds; not on the cess of war.
Foreheads of men have bled where no wounds were.
I am the enemy you killed, my friend.
I knew you in this dark; for so you frowned   40
Yesterday through me as you jabbed and killed.
I parried; but my hands were loath and cold.
Let us sleep now . . .'

(This poem was found among the author's papers. It ends on this
strange note.)

Another Version

Earth's wheels run oiled with blood. Forget we that.
Let us lie down and dig ourselves in thought.
Beauty is yours and you have mastery,
Wisdom is mine, and I have mystery.
We two will stay behind and keep our troth.   5
Let us forego men's minds that are brute's natures,
Let us not sup the blood which some say nurtures,
Be we not swift with swiftness of the tigress.
Let us break ranks from those who trek from progress.
Miss we the march of this retreating world   10
Into old citadels that are not walled.
Let us lie out and hold the open truth.
Then when their blood hath clogged the chariot wheels
We will go up and wash them from deep wells.
What though we sink from men as pitchers falling   15
Many shall raise us up to be their filling
Even from wells we sunk too deep for war
And filled by brows that bled where no wounds were.

Alternative line –
Even as One who bled where no wounds were.

Greater Love

Red lips are not so red
    As the stained stones kissed by the English dead.
Kindness of wooed and wooer
Seems shame to their love pure.
O Love, your eyes lose lure   5
    When I behold eyes blinded in my stead!

Your slender attitude
    Trembles not exquisite like limbs knife-skewed,
Rolling and rolling there
Where God seems not to care;   10
Till the fierce Love they bear
    Cramps them in death's extreme decrepitude.

Your voice sings not so soft, –
    Though even as wind murmuring through raftered loft, –
Your dear voice is not dear,   15
Gentle, and evening clear,
As theirs whom none now hear
    Now earth has stopped their piteous mouths that coughed.

Heart, you were never hot,
    Nor large, nor full like hearts made great with shot;   20
And though your hand be pale,
Paler are all which trail
Your cross through flame and hail:
    Weep, you may weep, for you may touch them not.

Apologia pro Poemate Meo

I, too, saw God through mud –
>The mud that cracked on cheeks when wretches smiled.
>War brought more glory to their eyes than blood,
>And gave their laughs more glee than shakes a child.

Merry it was to laugh there –   5
>Where death becomes absurd and life absurder.
>For power was on us as we slashed bones bare
>Not to feel sickness or remorse of murder.

I, too, have dropped off fear –
>Behind the barrage, dead as my platoon,   10
>And sailed my spirit surging, light and clear
>Past the entanglement where hopes lay strewn;

And witnessed exultation –
>Faces that used to curse me, scowl for scowl,
>Shine and lift up with passion of oblation,   15
>Seraphic for an hour; though they were foul.

I have made fellowships –
>Untold of happy lovers in old song.
>For love is not the binding of fair lips
>With the soft silk of eyes that look and long,   20

By Joy, whose ribbon slips, –
>But wound with war's hard wire whose stakes are strong;
>Bound with the bandage of the arm that drips;
>Knit in the welding of the rifle-thong.

I have perceived much beauty   25
>In the hoarse oaths that kept our courage straight;
>Heard music in the silentness of duty;
>Found peace where shell-storms spouted reddest spate.

Nevertheless, except you share
    With them in hell the sorrowful dark of hell,   30
    Whose world is but the trembling of a flare,
    And heaven but as the highway for a shell,

You shall not hear their mirth:
    You shall not come to think them well content
    By any jest of mine. These men are worth   35
    Your tears: You are not worth their merriment.

                        November 1917

The Show

My soul looked down from a vague height with Death,
As unremembering how I rose or why,
And saw a sad land, weak with sweats of dearth,
Gray, cratered like the moon with hollow woe,
And fitted with great pocks and scabs of plaques.   5

Across its beard, that horror of harsh wire,
There moved thin caterpillars, slowly uncoiled.
It seemed they pushed themselves to be as plugs
Of ditches, where they writhed and shrivelled, killed.

By them had slimy paths been trailed and scraped   10
Round myriad warts that might be little hills.

From gloom's last dregs these long-strung creatures crept,
And vanished out of dawn down hidden holes.

(And smell came up from those foul openings
As out of mouths, or deep wounds deepening.)   15

On dithering feet upgathered, more and more,
Brown strings towards strings of gray, with bristling spines,
All migrants from green fields, intent on mire.

Those that were gray, of more abundant spawns,
Ramped on the rest and ate them and were eaten.   20

I saw their bitten backs curve, loop, and straighten,
I watched those agonies curl, lift, and flatten.

Whereat, in terror what that sight might mean,
I reeled and shivered earthward like a feather.

And Death fell with me, like a deepening moan.   25

And He, picking a manner of worm, which half had hid
Its bruises in the earth, but crawled no further,
Showed me its feet, the feet of many men,
And the fresh-severed head of it, my head.

Mental Cases

Who are these? Why sit they here in twilight?
Wherefore rock they, purgatorial shadows,
Drooping tongues from jaws that slob their relish,
Baring teeth that leer like skulls' tongues wicked?
Stroke on stroke of pain, – but what slow panic,   5
Gouged these chasms round their fretted sockets?
Ever from their hair and through their hand palms
Misery swelters. Surely we have perished
Sleeping, and walk hell; but who these hellish?

– These are men whose minds the Dead have ravished.   10
Memory fingers in their hair of murders,
Multitudinous murders they once witnessed.
Wading sloughs of flesh these helpless wander,
Treading blood from lungs that had loved laughter.
Always they must see these things and hear them,   15
Batter of guns and shatter of flying muscles,
Carnage incomparable and human squander
Rucked too thick for these men's extrication.

Therefore still their eyeballs shrink tormented
Back into their brains, because on their sense   20
Sunlight seems a bloodsmear; night comes blood-black;
Dawn breaks open like a wound that bleeds afresh
– Thus their heads wear this hilarious, hideous,
Awful falseness of set-smiling corpses.
– Thus their hands are plucking at each other;   25
Picking at the rope-knouts of their scourging;
Snatching after us who smote them, brother,
Pawing us who dealt them war and madness.

Parable of the Old Men and the Young

So Abram rose, and clave the wood, and went,
And took the fire with him, and a knife.
And as they sojourned both of them together,
Isaac the first-born spake and said, My Father,
Behold the preparations, fire and iron,   5
But where the lamb for this burnt-offering?
Then Abram bound the youth with belts and straps,
And builded parapets and trenches there,
And stretchèd forth the knife to slay his son.
When lo! an angel called him out of heaven,   10
Saying, Lay not thy hand upon the lad,
Neither do anything to him. Behold,
A ram caught in a thicket by its horns;
Offer the Ram of Pride instead of him.
But the old man would not so, but slew his son. . . .   15

Arms and the Boy

Let the boy try along this bayonet-blade
How cold steel is, and keen with hunger of blood;
Blue with all malice, like a madman's flash;
And thinly drawn with famishing for flesh.

Lend him to stroke these blind, blunt bullet-heads   5
Which long to muzzle in the hearts of lads.
Or give him cartridges of fine zinc teeth,
Sharp with the sharpness of grief and death.

For his teeth seem for laughing round an apple.
There lurk no claws behind his fingers supple;   10
And God will grow no talons at his heels,
Nor antlers through the thickness of his curls.

Anthem for Doomed Youth

What passing-bells for these who die as cattle?
    Only the monstrous anger of the guns.
    Only the stuttering rifles' rapid rattle
Can patter out their hasty orisons.
No mockeries for them; no prayers nor bells,   5
Nor any voice of mourning save the choirs, –
The shrill, demented choirs of wailing shells;
And bugles calling for them from sad shires.

What candles may be held to speed them all?
    Not in the hands of boys, but in their eyes   10
Shall shine the holy glimmers of goodbyes.
    The pallor of girls' brows shall be their pall;
Their flowers the tenderness of patient minds,
And each slow dusk a drawing-down of blinds.

The Send-off

Down the close, darkening lanes they sang their way
To the siding-shed,
And lined the train with faces grimly gay.

Their breasts were stuck all white with wreath and spray
As men's are, dead. 5

Dull porters watched them, and a casual tramp
Stood staring hard,
Sorry to miss them from the upland camp.
Then, unmoved, signals nodded, and a lamp
Winked to the guard. 10

So secretly, like wrongs hushed-up, they went.
They were not ours:
We never heard to which front these were sent.

Nor there if they yet mock what women meant
Who gave them flowers. 15

Shall they return to beatings of great bells
In wild trainloads?
A few, a few, too few for drums and yells,
May creep back, silent, to still village wells
Up half-known roads. 20

Insensibility

I

Happy are men who yet before they are killed
Can let their veins run cold.
Whom no compassion fleers
Or makes their feet
Sore on the alleys cobbled with their brothers.   5
The front line withers,
But they are troops who fade, not flowers
For poets' tearful fooling:
Men, gaps for filling
Losses who might have fought   10
Longer; but no one bothers.

II

And some cease feeling
Even themselves or for themselves.
Dullness best solves
The tease and doubt of shelling,   15
And Chance's strange arithmetic
Comes simpler than the reckoning of their shilling.
They keep no check on Armies' decimation.

III

Happy are these who lose imagination:
They have enough to carry with ammunition.   20
Their spirit drags no pack.
Their old wounds save with cold can not more ache.
Having seen all things red,
Their eyes are rid
Of the hurt of the colour of blood for ever.   25
And terror's first constriction over,
Their hearts remain small drawn.
Their senses in some scorching cautery of battle
Now long since ironed,
Can laugh among the dying, unconcerned.   30

IV

Happy the soldier home, with not a notion
How somewhere, every dawn, some men attack,
And many sighs are drained.
Happy the lad whose mind was never trained:
His days are worth forgetting more than not.   35
He sings along the march
Which we march taciturn, because of dusk,
The long, forlorn, relentless trend
From larger day to huger night.

V

We wise, who with a thought besmirch   40
Blood over all our soul,
How should we see our task
But through his blunt and lashless eyes?
Alive, he is not vital overmuch;
Dying, not mortal overmuch;   45
Nor sad, nor proud,
Nor curious at all.
He cannot tell
Old men's placidity from his.

VI

But cursed are dullards whom no cannon stuns,   50
That they should be as stones.
Wretched are they, and mean
With paucity that never was simplicity.
By choice they made themselves immune
To pity and whatever mourns in man   55
Before the last sea and the hapless stars;
Whatever mourns when many leave these shores;
Whatever shares
The eternal reciprocity of tears.

Dulce et Decorum est

Bent double, like old beggars under sacks,
Knock-kneed, coughing like hags, we cursed through sludge,
Till on the haunting flares we turned our backs,
And towards our distant rest began to trudge.
Men marched asleep. Many had lost their boots,   5
But limped on, blood-shod. All went lame, all blind;
Drunk with fatigue; deaf even to the hoots
Of gas-shells dropping softly behind.

Gas! GAS! Quick, boys! – An ecstasy of fumbling
Fitting the clumsy helmets just in time,   10
But someone still was yelling out and stumbling
And flound'ring like a man in fire or lime. –
Dim through the misty panes and thick green light,
As under a green sea, I saw him drowning.

In all my dreams before my helpless sight   15
He plunges at me, guttering, choking, drowning.

If in some smothering dreams, you too could pace
Behind the wagon that we flung him in,
And watch the white eyes writhing in his face,
His hanging face, like a devil's sick of sin,   20
If you could hear, at every jolt, the blood
Come gargling from the froth-corrupted lungs
Bitten as the cud
Of vile, incurable sores on innocent tongues, –
My friend, you would not tell with such high zest   25
To children ardent for some desperate glory,
The old Lie: *Dulce et decorum est*
Pro patria mori.

The Sentry

We'd found an old Boche dug-out, and he knew,
And gave us hell, for shell on frantic shell
Hammered on top, but never quite burst through.
Rain, guttering down in waterfalls of slime
Kept slush waist high, that rising hour by hour,   5
Choked up the steps too thick with clay to climb.
What murk of air remained stank old, and sour
With fumes of whizz-bangs, and the smell of men
Who'd lived there years, and left their curse in the den,
If not their corpses. . . .
           There we herded from the blast   10
Of whizz-bangs, but one found our door at last.
Buffeting eyes and breath, snuffing the candles.
And thud! flump! thud! down the steep steps came thumping
And splashing in the flood, deluging muck –
The sentry's body; then his rifle, handles   15
Of old Boche bombs, and mud in ruck on ruck.
We dredged him up, for killed, until he whined
'O sir, my eyes – I'm blind – I'm blind, I'm blind!'
Coaxing, I held a flame against his lids
And said if he could see the least blurred light   20
He was not blind; in time he'd get all right.
'I can't,' he sobbed. Eyeballs, huge-bulged like squids
Watch my dreams still; but I forgot him there
In posting next for duty, and sending a scout
To beg a stretcher somewhere, and floundering about   25
To other posts under the shrieking air.

Those other wretches, how they bled and spewed,
And one who would have drowned himself for good, –
I try not to remember these things now.
Let dread hark back for one word only: how   30
Half-listening to that sentry's moans and jumps,
And the wild chattering of his broken teeth,
Renewed most horribly whenever crumps

Pummelled the roof and slogged the air beneath –
Through the dense din, I say, we heard him shout   35
'I see your lights!' But ours had long died out.

The Dead-Beat

He dropped, – more sullenly than wearily,
Lay stupid like a cod, heavy like meat,
And none of us could kick him to his feet;
Just blinked at my revolver, blearily;
– Didn't appear to know a war was on,   5
Or see the blasted trench at which he stared.
'I'll do 'em in,' he whined, 'If this hand's spared,
I'll murder them, I will.'

        A low voice said,
'It's Blighty, p'raps, he sees; his pluck's all gone,
Dreaming of all the valiant, that *aren't* dead: 10
Bold uncles, smiling ministerially;
Maybe his brave young wife, getting her fun
In some new home, improved materially.
It's not these stiffs have crazed him; nor the Hun.'

We sent him down at last, out of the way.   15
Unwounded; – stout lad, too, before that strafe.
Malingering? Stretcher-bearers winked, 'Not half!'

Next day I heard the Doc's well-whiskied laugh:
'That scum you sent last night soon died. Hooray!'

Exposure

I

Our brains ache, in the merciless iced east winds that knife us . . .
Wearied we keep awake because the night is silent . . .
Low drooping flares confuse our memory of the salient . . .
Worried by silence, sentries whisper, curious, nervous,
      But nothing happens.   5

Watching, we hear the mad gusts tugging on the wire.
Like twitching agonies of men among its brambles.
Northward incessantly, the flickering gunnery rumbles,
Far off, like a dull rumour of some other war.
      What are we doing here?   10

The poignant misery of dawn begins to grow . . .
We only know war lasts, rain soaks, and clouds sag stormy.
Dawn massing in the east her melancholy army
Attacks once more in ranks on shivering ranks of gray,
      But nothing happens.   15

Sudden successive flights of bullets streak the silence.
Less deadly than the air that shudders black with snow,
With sidelong flowing flakes that flock, pause and renew,
We watch them wandering up and down the wind's
  nonchalance,
      But nothing happens.   20

II

Pale flakes with lingering stealth come feeling for our faces –
We cringe in holes, back on forgotten dreams, and stare, snow-
  dazed,
Deep into grassier ditches. So we drowse, sun-dozed,
Littered with blossoms trickling where the blackbird fusses.
      Is it that we are dying?   25

Slowly our ghosts drag home: glimpsing the sunk fires glozed
With crusted dark-red jewels; crickets jingle there;
For hours the innocent mice rejoice: the house is theirs;
Shutters and doors all closed: on us the doors are closed –
       We turn back to our dying.   30

Since we believe not otherwise can kind fires burn;
Now ever suns smile true on child, or field, or fruit.
For God's invincible spring our love is made afraid;
Therefore, not loath, we lie out here; therefore were born,
       For love of God seems dying.   35

Tonight, His frost will fasten on this mud and us,
Shrivelling many hands and puckering foreheads crisp.
The burying-party, picks and shovels in their shaking grasp,
Pause over half-known faces. All their eyes are ice,
       But nothing happens.   40

Spring Offensive

Halted against the shade of a last hill,
They fed, and, lying easy, were at ease
And, finding comfortable chests and knees
Carelessly slept. But many there stood still
To face the stark, blank sky beyond the ridge,　　　　　5
Knowing their feet had come to the end of the world.

Marvelling they stood, and watched the long grass swirled
By the May breeze, murmurous with wasp and midge,
For though the summer oozed into their veins
Like the injected drug for their bones' pains,　　　　　10
Sharp on their souls hung the imminent line of grass,
Fearfully flashed the sky's mysterious glass.

Hour after hour they ponder the warm field –
And the far valley behind, where the buttercups
Had blessed with gold their slow boots coming up,　　　　　15
Where even the little brambles would not yield,
But clutched and clung to them like sorrowing hands;
They breathe like trees unstirred.

Till like a cold gust thrilled the little word
At which each body and its soul begird　　　　　20
And tighten them for battle. No alarms
Of bugles, no high flags, no clamorous haste –
Only a lift and flare of eyes that faced
The sun, like a friend with whom their love is done.
O larger shone that smile against the sun, –　　　　　25
Mightier than his whose bounty these have spurned.

So, soon they topped the hill, and raced together
Over an open stretch of herb and heather
Exposed. And instantly the whole sky burned
With fury against them; and soft sudden cups　　　　　30

Opened in thousands for their blood; and the green slopes
Chasmed and steepened sheer to infinite space.

Of them who running on that last high place
Leapt to swift unseen bullets, or went up
On the hot blast and fury of hell's upsurge,   35
Or plunged and fell away past this world's verge,
Some say God caught them even before they fell.

But what say such as from existence' brink
Ventured but drave too swift to sink.
The few who rushed in the body to enter hell,   40
And there out-fiending all its fiends and flames
With superhuman inhumanities,
Long-famous glories, immemorial shames –
And crawling slowly back, have by degrees
Regained cool peaceful air in wonder –   45
Why speak they not of comrades that went under?

The Chances

I mind as 'ow the night afore that show
Us five got talking, – we was in the know,
'Over the top tomorrer; boys, we're for it,
First wave we are, first ruddy wave; that's tore it.'
'Ah well,' says Jimmy, – an' 'e's seen some scrappin' –   5
'There ain't more nor five things as can 'appen;
Ye get knocked out; else wounded – bad or cushy;
Scuppered; or nowt except yer feeling mushy.'

One of us got the knock-out, blown to chops.
T'other was hurt, like, losin' both 'is props.   10
An' one, to use the word of 'ypocrites,
'Ad the misfortoon to be took by Fritz.
Now me, I wasn't scratched, praise God Almighty
(Though next time please I'll thank 'im for a blighty),
But poor young Jim, 'e's livin' an' 'e's not;   15
'E reckoned 'e'd five chances, an' 'e's 'ad;
'E's wounded, killed, and pris'ner, all the lot –
The ruddy lot all rolled in one. Jim's mad.

S.I.W.

I will to the King,
And offer him consolation in his trouble,
For that man there has set his teeth to die,
And being one that hates obedience,
Discipline, and orderliness of life,
I cannot mourn him.

W. B. Yeats

Patting goodbye, doubtless they told the lad
He'd always show the Hun a brave man's face;
Father would sooner him dead than in disgrace, –
Was proud to see him going, aye, and glad.
Perhaps his Mother whimpered how she'd fret   5
Until he got a nice, safe wound to nurse.
Sisters would wish girls too could shoot, charge, curse, . . .
Brothers – would send his favourite cigarette,
Each week, month after month, they wrote the same,
Thinking him sheltered in some Y.M. Hut,   10
Where once an hour a bullet missed its aim
And misses teased the hunger of his brain.
His eyes grew old with wincing, and his hand
Reckless with ague. Courage leaked, as sand
From the best sandbags after years of rain.   15
But never leave, wound, fever, trench-foot, shock,
Untrapped the wretch. And death seemed still withheld
For torture of lying machinally shelled,
At the pleasure of this world's Powers who'd run amok.

He'd seen men shoot their hands, on night patrol,   20
Their people never knew. Yet they were vile.
'Death sooner than dishonour, that's the style!'
So Father said.

        One dawn, our wire patrol
Carried him. This time, Death had not missed.

We could do nothing, but wipe his bleeding cough.   25
Could it be accident? – Rifles go off . . .
Not sniped? No. (Later they found the English ball.)

It was the reasoned crisis of his soul.
Against the fires that would not burn him whole
But kept him for death's perjury and scoff   30
And life's half-promising, and both their riling.

With him they buried the muzzle his teeth had kissed,
And truthfully wrote the Mother 'Tim died smiling.'

Futility

Move him into the sun –
Gently its touch awoke him once,
At home, whispering of fields unsown.
Always it woke him, even in France,
Until this morning and this snow.   5
If anything might rouse him now
The kind old sun will know.

Think how it wakes the seeds –
Woke, once, the clays of a cold star.
Are limbs so dear-achieved, are sides   10
Full-nerved, – still warm, – too hard to stir?
Was it for this the clay grew tall?
– O what made fatuous sunbeams toil
To break earth's sleep at all?

Smile, Smile, Smile

Head to limp head, the sunk-eyed wounded scanned
Yesterday's Mail; the casualties (typed small)
And (large) Vast Booty from our Latest Haul.
Also, they read of Cheap Homes, not yet planned;
For, said the paper, 'When this war is done   5
The men's first instinct will be making homes.
Meanwhile their foremost need is aerodromes,
It being certain war has just begun.
Peace would do wrong to our undying dead, –
The sons we offered might regret they died   10
If we got nothing lasting in their stead.
We must be solidly indemnified.
Though all be worthy Victory which all bought,
We rulers sitting in this ancient spot
Would wrong our very selves if we forgot   15
The greatest glory will be theirs who fought,
Who kept this nation in integrity.
Nation? – The half-limbed readers did not chafe
But smiled at one another curiously
Like secret men who know their secret safe.   20
This is the thing they know and never speak,
That England one by one had fled to France
(Not many elsewhere now save under France).
Pictures of these broad smiles appear each week,
And people in whose voice real feeling rings   25
Say: How they smile! They're happy now, poor things.

23 September 1918

Conscious

His fingers wake, and flutter up the bed.
His eyes come open with a pull of will,
Helped by the yellow may-flowers by his head.
A blind-cord drawls across the window-sill . . .
How smooth the floor of the ward is! what a rug!   5
And who's that talking, somewhere out of sight?
Why are they laughing? What's inside that jug?
'Nurse! Doctor!' 'Yes; all right, all right.'

But sudden dusk bewilders all the air –
There seems no time to want a drink of water.   10
Nurse looks so far away. And everywhere
Music and roses burnt through crimson slaughter.
Cold; cold; he's cold; and yet so hot:
And there's no light to see the voices by –
No time to dream, and ask – he knows not what.   15

A Terre

(Being the philosophy of many Soldiers)

Sit on the bed; I'm blind, and three parts shell,
Be careful; can't shake hands now; never shall.
Both arms have mutinied against me – brutes.
My fingers fidget like ten idle brats.

I tried to peg out soldierly – no use!   5
One dies of war like any old disease.
This bandage feels like pennies on my eyes.
I have my medals? – Discs to make eyes close.
My glorious ribbons? – Ripped from my own back
In scarlet shreds. (That's for your poetry book.)   10

A short life and a merry one, my brick!
We used to say we'd hate to live dead old, –
Yet now . . . I'd willingly be puffy, bald,
And patriotic. Buffers catch from boys
At least the jokes hurled at them. I suppose   15
Little I'd ever teach a son, but hitting,
Shooting, war, hunting, all the arts of hurting.
Well, that's what I learnt, – that, and making money.
Your fifty years ahead seem none too many?
Tell me how long I've got? God! For one year   20
To help myself to nothing more than air!
One Spring! Is one too good to spare, too long?
Spring wind would work its own way to my lung,
And grow me legs as quick as lilac-shoots.
My servant's lamed, but listen how he shouts!   25
When I'm lugged out, he'll still be good for that.
Here in this mummy-case, you know, I've thought
How well I might have swept his floors for ever,
I'd ask no night off when the bustle's over,
Enjoying so the dirt. Who's prejudiced   30
Against a grimed hand when his own's quite dust,

Less live than specks that in the sun-shafts turn,
Less warm than dust that mixes with arms' tan?
I'd love to be a sweep, now, black as Town,
Yes, or a muckman. Must I be his load?   35
O Life, Life, let me breathe, – a dug-out rat!
Not worse than ours the existences rats lead –
Nosing along at night down some safe vat,
They find a shell-proof home before they rot.
Dead men may envy living mites in cheese,   40
Or good germs even. Microbes have their joys,
And subdivide, and never come to death,
Certainly flowers have the easiest time on earth.
'I shall be one with nature, herb, and stone.'
Shelley would tell me. Shelley would be stunned;   45
The dullest Tommy hugs that fancy now.
'Pushing up daisies,' is their creed, you know.
To grain, then, go my fat, to buds my sap,
For all the usefulness there is in soap.
D'you think the Boche will ever stew man-soup?   50
Some day, no doubt, if . . .
                          Friend, be very sure
I shall be better off with plants that share
More peaceably the meadow and the shower.
Soft rains will touch me, – as they could touch once,
And nothing but the sun shall make me ware.   55
Your guns may crash around me. I'll not hear;
Or, if I wince, I shall not know I wince.
Don't take my soul's poor comfort for your jest.
Soldiers may grow a soul when turned to fronds,
But here the thing's best left at home with friends.   60

My soul's a little grief, grappling your chest,
To climb your throat on sobs; easily chased
On other sighs and wiped by fresher winds.

Carry my crying spirit till it's weaned
To do without what blood remained these wounds.   65

Wild with all Regrets

(Another version of 'A Terre')

TO SIEGFRIED SASSOON

My arms have mutinied against me – brutes!
My fingers fidget like ten idle brats,
My back's been stiff for hours, damned hours.
Death never gives his squad a Stand-at-ease.
I can't read. There: it's no use. Take your book.   5
A short life and a merry one, my buck!
We said we'd hate to grow dead old. But now,
Not to live old seems awful: not to renew
My boyhood with my boys, and teach 'em hitting,
Shooting and hunting, – all the arts of hurting!   10
– Well, that's what I learnt. That, and making money.
Your fifty years in store seem none too many;
But I've five minutes. God! For just two years
To help myself to this good air of yours!
One Spring! Is one too hard to spare? Too long?   15
Spring air would find its own way to my lung,
And grow me legs as quick as lilac-shoots.

Yes, there's the orderly. He'll change the sheets
When I'm lugged out, oh, couldn't I do that?
Here in this coffin of a bed, I've thought   20
I'd like to kneel and sweep his floors for ever, –
And ask no nights off when the bustle's over,
For I'd enjoy the dirt; who's prejudiced
Against a grimed hand when his own's quite dust, –
Less live than specks that in the sun-shafts turn?   25
Dear dust, – in rooms, on roads, on faces' tan!
I'd love to be a sweep's boy, black as Town;
Yes, or a muckman. Must I be his load?
A flea would do. If one chap wasn't bloody,
Or went stone-cold, I'd find another body.   30

Which I shan't manage now. Unless it's yours.
I shall stay in you, friend, for some few hours.

You'll feel my heavy spirit chill your chest,
And climb your throat on sobs, until it's chased
On sighs, and wiped from off your lips by wind.   35

I think on your rich breathing, brother, I'll be weaned
To do without what blood remained me from my wound.

5 December 1917

Disabled

He sat in a wheeled chair, waiting for dark,
And shivered in his ghastly suit of grey,
Legless, sewn short at elbow. Through the park
Voices of boys rang saddening like a hymn,
Voices of play and pleasure after day,   5
Till gathering sleep had mothered them from him.

About this time Town used to swing so gay
When glow-lamps budded in the light-blue trees
And girls glanced lovelier as the air grew dim,
– In the old times, before he threw away his knees.   10
Now he will never feel again how slim
Girls' waists are, or how warm their subtle hands,
All of them touch him like some queer disease.

There was an artist silly for his face,
For it was younger than his youth, last year.   15
Now he is old; his back will never brace;
He's lost his colour very far from here,
Poured it down shell-holes till the veins ran dry,
And half his lifetime lapsed in the hot race,
And leap of purple spurted from his thigh.   20
One time he liked a bloodsmear down his leg,
After the matches carried shoulder-high.
It was after football, when he'd drunk a peg,
He thought he'd better join. He wonders why . . .
Someone had said he'd look a god in kilts.   25

That's why; and maybe, too, to please his Meg,
Aye, that was it, to please the giddy jilts,
He asked to join. He didn't have to beg;
Smiling they wrote his lie; aged nineteen years.
Germans he scarcely thought of; and no fears   30
Of Fear came yet. He thought of jewelled hilts
For daggers in plaid socks; of smart salutes;

And care of arms; and leave; and pay arrears;
Esprit de corps; and hints for young recruits.
And soon, he was drafted out with drums and cheers.   35

Some cheered him home, but not as crowds cheer Goal.
Only a solemn man who brought him fruits
Thanked him; and then inquired about his soul.
Now, he will spend a few sick years in Institutes,
And do what things the rules consider wise,   40
And take whatever pity they may dole.
Tonight he noticed how the women's eyes
Passed from him to the strong men that were whole.
How cold and late it is! Why don't they come
And put him into bed? Why don't they come?   45

The End

After the blast of lightning from the east,
The flourish of loud clouds, the Chariot throne,
After the drums of time have rolled and ceased
And from the bronze west long retreat is blown,

Shall Life renew these bodies? Of a truth   5
All death will he annul, all tears assuage?
Or fill these void veins full again with youth
And wash with an immortal water age?

When I do ask white Age, he saith not so, –
'My head hangs weighed with snow.'   10
And when I hearken to the Earth she saith
'My fiery heart sinks aching. It is death.
Mine ancient scars shall not be glorified
Nor my titanic tears the seas be dried.'

Other Related Poems

Song of Songs

Sing me at morn but only with your laugh:
Even as Spring that laugheth into leaf;
Even as Love that laugheth after Life.

Sing me but only with your speech all day,
As voluble leaflets do; let viols die;   5
The least word of your lips is melody!

Sing me at eve but only with your sigh!
Like lifting seas it solaceth; breathe so,
Slowly and low, the sense that no songs say.

Sing me at midnight with your murmurous heart!   10
Let youth's immortal-moaning chords be heard
Throbbing through you, and sobbing, unsubdued.

The Next War

War's a joke for me and you,
When we know such dreams are true.

Sassoon

Out there, we've walked quite friendly up to Death;
  Sat down and eaten with him, cool and bland, –
  Pardoned his spilling mess-tins in our hand.
We've sniffed the green thick odour of his breath, –
Our eyes wept, but our courage didn't writhe.   5
  He's spat at us with bullets and he's coughed
  Shrapnel. We chorused when he sang aloft;
We whistled while he shaved us with his scythe.

Oh, Death was never enemy of ours!
  We laughed at him, we leagued with him, old chum.   10
No soldier's paid to kick against his powers.
  We laughed, knowing that better men would come,
And greater wars: when each proud fighter brags
He wars on Death – for Life; not men – for flags.

Miners

There was a whispering in my hearth,
   A sigh of the coal,
Grown wistful of a former earth
   It might recall.

I listened for a tale of leaves
   And smothered ferns,
Frond-forests, and the low sly lives
   Before the fawns.

My fire might show steam-phantoms simmer
   From Time's old cauldron,
Before the birds made nests in summer,
   Or men had children.

But the coals were murmuring of their mine,
   And moans down there
Of boys that slept wry sleep, and men
   Writhing for air.

I saw white bones in the cinder-shard,
   Bones without number.
For many hearts with coal are charred,
   And few remember.

I thought of all that worked dark pits
   Of war, and died
Digging the rock where Death reputes
   Peace lies indeed:

Comforted years will sit soft-chaired,
   In rooms of amber,
The years will stretch their hands, well-cheered
   By our life's ember;

The centuries will burn rich loads
  With which we groaned,   30
Whose warmth shall lull their dreaming lids,
  While songs are crooned;
But they will not dream of us poor lads,
  Lost in the ground.

Hospital Barge

Budging the sluggard ripples of the Somme
A barge round old Cèrisy slowly slewed.
Softly her engines down the current screwed,
And chuckled softly with contented hum,
Till fairy tinklings struck their crooning dumb.   5
The waters rumpling at the stern subdued:
The lock-gate took her bulging amplitude:
Gently from out the gurgling lock she swum.

One reading by that calm bank shaded eyes
To watch her lessening westward quietly.   10
Then, as she neared the bend, her funnel screamed.
And in that long lamentation made him wise
How unto Avilon in agony
Kings passed in the dark barge which Merlin dreamed.

Asleep

Under his helmet, up against his pack,
After so many days of work and waking
Sleep took him by the brow and laid him back.

There, in the happy no-time of his sleeping,
Death took him by the heart. There heaved a quaking   5
Of frustrate life, like child within him leaping . . .
Then chest and sleepy arms once more fell slack.

And soon the slow stray blood comes creeping
From the intrusive lead, like ants on track.

                    *   *   *   *

Whether his deeper sleep lie shaded by the shaking   10
Of great wings, and the thoughts of stars,
High-pillowed on calm clouds of God's making,
Above these clouds, these rains, these sleets of lead,
And these winds' scimitars;
– Or whether yet his thin and sodden head   15
Confuses more and more with the low mould,
His hair being one with the grey grass
Of finished fields, and wire-scrags rusty-old, . . .
Who knows? Who hopes? Who troubles? Let it pass!
He sleeps. He sleeps less tremulous, less cold   20
Than we who wake, and waking say, Alas!

Notes

RUPERT BROOKE

1914 & Other Poems

1914 and Other Poems was published by Sidgwick & Jackson in June 1915. Its contents were prefaced by a brief summary of Brooke's life emphasising his military experience, an acknowledgement of previous publication and the note: 'The Author had thought of publishing a volume of poems this spring, but did not prepare the present book for publication.' It was in fact Brooke's friend Edward Marsh who was responsible for the volume's assembly and arrangement, although the reverse chronological order was modelled on Brooke's practice in *Poems*. Reviews of it were unanimously favourable and, within a week of publication, it had gone through three impressions. By May 1931, it had sold some 37,000 copies.

pp. 3–7 1914: first published in *New Numbers*, Vol. I, No. 4 (December 1914), pp. 165–9. A separate edition of these sonnets published by Sidgwick & Jackson seven months after Brooke's death had, by 1926, sold over 8,000 copies.

p. 8 *The Treasure*: *ibid.*, p. 164.

p. 9 *Tiare Tahiti*: first published in *New Numbers*, Vol. I, No. 3 (August 1914), pp. 109–11. The title is Polynesian for flower of Tahiti. **1 Mamua:** according to Christopher Hassall in *Rupert Brooke: A Biography* (1964), the Mamua to whom this poem is addressed was a Polynesian woman called Taatamata whom Brooke fell in love with during his stay on Tahiti. **11 Pupure:** Polynesian for fair and, according to Brooke, his nickname amongst the islanders. **31–5 Miri ... Teïpo ... Matua ... Teüra:** Polynesian proper names. **56 *Taü here*:** from the evidence of a letter from Brooke to Cathleen Nesbitt written in April 1914, this seems to be a term of affection equivalent to the Italian *Mia cara*. **Papeete:** the principal town of Tahiti.

p. 12 *Retrospect*: *ibid.*, pp. 112–15. **Mataiea:** the village in which Taatamata lived.

p. 14 *The Great Lover*: *ibid.*, pp. 114–16.

p. 17 *Heaven*: 22 Squamous: scaly or scalelike.

p. 19 *There's Wisdom in Women*: first published in *The New Statesman*, 18 October 1913, p. 51.

p. 20 *He wonders whether to praise or to blame her*: first published in *Poetry & Drama*, Vol. I, No. 4 (December 1913), p. 404.

p. 21 *A Memory*: first published in *New Numbers*, Vol. I, No. 1 (February 1914), p. 28.

p. 22 *One Day*: *ibid.*, p. 29.

p. 23 *Waikiki*: first published in *New Numbers*, Vol. I, No. 3 (August 1914), p. 117. Waikiki is a resort in Honolulu, Hawaii. **3 *eukaleli*:** literally meaning 'jumping flea', this is a small four-stringed Hawaiian guitar.

p. 24 *Hauntings*: *ibid.*, p. 118. **11 Lethean:** according to Greek mythology, Lethe was a river in Hades that induced forgetfulness of the past.

p. 25 *Sonnet*: first published in *New Numbers*, Vol. I, No. 1 (February 1914), p. 27. The Society for Psychical Research (see sub-title) was founded in 1882 by a group of scientists and philosophers from Trinity College, Cambridge. Their aims, as laid out in their *Proceedings*, were 'to examine without prejudice or presupposition and in a scientific spirit those faculties of man, real or supposed, which appear inexplicable in terms of any generally recognised hypotheses'.

p. 26 *Clouds*: first published in *Poetry & Drama*, Vol. I, No. 4 (December 1913), p. 405.

p. 27 *Mutability*: first published in *New Numbers*, Vol. I, No. 1 (February 1914), p. 30. **4 *Æterna corpora*:** Latin for eternal or everlasting body. **Makaweli:** a village on the Hawaiian island of Kauai.

p. 29 *The Busy Heart*: first published in *The Blue Review*, Vol. I, No. 3 (July 1913), p. 150.

p. 30 *Love*: *ibid.*, p. 149.

p. 31 *Unfortunate*: first published in *The Poetry Review*, Vol. I, No. 11 (November 1912), p. 507.

p. 32 *The Chilterns*: first published in *The New Statesman*, 3 May 1913, p.

113. The Chiltern Hills range across Oxfordshire, Buckinghamshire, Bedfordshire and Hertfordshire. **8 Wendover:** the Chilterns reach their highest point – 276 metres – near Wendover in Buckinghamshire. **9 Tring and Lilley Hoo:** Tring is a town in Hertfordshire; Lilley Hoo is a village in Hertfordshire, near Luton.

p. 35 *The Night Journey*: first published in *Rhythm*, Vol. II, No. 12 (November 1913), p. 338.

p. 36 *Song*: first published in *The Poetry Review*, Vol. I, No. 11 (November 1912), p. 504.

p. 37 *Beauty and Beauty*: *ibid.*, p. 506.

p. 38 *The Way that Lovers use*: first published in *Poetry & Drama*, Vol. I, No. 4 (December 1913), p. 405.

p. 39 *Mary and Gabriel*: first published in *The Poetry Review*, Vol. I, No. 11 (November 1912), pp. 505–6. The most complete account of the Annunciation can be found in Luke 1: 26–38.

p. 41 *The Funeral of Youth: Threnody*: first published in *Poetry & Drama*, Vol. I, No. 4 (December 1913), pp. 402–3. Threnody is the classical Greek name for a song of mourning, especially a lamentation for the dead.

p. 43 *The Old Vicarage, Grantchester*: first published as 'Fragments from a Poem to be entitled "The Sentimental Exile" ' in *Basileon H (Being the Seventh Book of King's)*, Number 14 (June 1912), pp. 3–4. It appeared in full with its more familiar title in *The Poetry Review*, Vol. I, No. 11 (November 1912), pp. 507–9, and was published in book form in *Georgian Poetry 1911–1912* (London: The Poetry Bookshop, 1912), pp. 33–5. **Café des Westens:** Brooke's favourite haunt during his stay in Berlin. **4 the pink:** a perennial wild flower. **17 *Du lieber Gott!*:** a German exclamation literally meaning 'Dear God!' **21 *Temperamentvoll*:** German for vivacious or lively. **30 Hesper:** a contraction of Hesperus, an evening star. **31 Meads:** meadows. **Haslingfield and Coton:** like the places named later in the poem, these are villages in Cambridgeshire. **32 *das Betreten's* not *verboten*:** German and English for 'entry is not forbidden'. **33** εἴθε γενοίμην: Greek for 'would I were!' **38 Faun:** a half-goat, half-human Roman pastoral deity. **40 Naiad:** a Greek water-nymph. **41 Goat-foot:** Pan, the Greek god of shepherds and flocks, who was also half-goat, half-human. **52 Hellespont, or Styx:** rivers in classical mythology. The Hellespont, the ancient name for the Dardanelles, is celebrated in the story of Hero and Leander; the Styx is the river of hate that flowed nine times

around the infernal regions. **53 Dan Chaucer:** Geoffrey Chaucer (*c.*
1343–1400), best known for his long narrative poem, *The Canterbury Tales*.
The action in one of these, *The Reeve's Tale*, takes place down stream from
Grantchester at a mill in 'Trompyngtoun'. **55 Tennyson:** Alfred, Lord
Tennyson (1809–92) studied at Trinity College, Cambridge in the late
1820s. 'The Miller's Daughter', published in *Poems* (1842), seems to have
been partly inspired by Chaucer's *Reeve's Tale*. **104 bosky:** wooded or
bushy. **126 Anadyomene:** literally meaning rising, this was the title given
to portrayals of Aphrodite or Venus when she was shown being born from
the sea in classical art. **139 Stands the Church clock at ten to three?:**
Christopher Hassall notes that the church clock at Grantchester *was*
actually stuck for most of 1911, but at half-past three.

Other Related Poems

Following the success of *1914 and Other Poems*, Edward Marsh was asked by
Sidgwick & Jackson to produce a more comprehensive edition of Brooke's
work. *The Collected Poems of Rupert Brooke: With a Memoir*, published in July
1918, contained a number of newly discovered texts, several of which
would have been appropriate inclusions in *1914 and Other Poems*. A second
edition of *The Collected Poems* appeared in 1928.

p. 47 Fafaïa: first published in *The London Mercury*, Vol. XVIII, No. 104
(June 1928), p. 126, with a footnote by E[dward] M[arsh]: 'This poem,
which Rupert Brooke sent me in a letter from the South Seas, has been
mislaid ever since, and only now come to light among my papers.'
Reprinted in *The South Seas* section of the edition of *The Collected Poems*,
p. 129. Fafaïa is either a Samoan proper name or a reference to *fiafia*, the
local name for a display of music and dancing. Brooke describes witnessing
such an event in a letter to Cathleen Nesbitt of November 1913, although
there he calls it a *siva-siva*. **Saanapu:** a village in Western Samoa.

p. 48 A Song: found in Brooke's notebook after his death and first
published in the 1918 edition of *The Collected Poems*, p. 150. This lyric,
retitled 'The Dance' in the 1928 edition, was written for Brooke's old
schoolfriend and fellow-officer in the Hood Battalion, the composer W.
Denis Browne (1888–1915).

p. 49 Fragment: *ibid.*, p. 149. Traditionally thought of as Brooke's last
poem. **11 pashed:** dashed to pieces.

WILFRED OWEN

Poems by Wilfred Owen

Poems by Wilfred Owen was first published by Chatto & Windus in December 1920. Two years earlier, Osbert and Edith Sitwell had approached Owen for contributions to their 1918 *Wheels* anthology, but by the time he had submitted eight of his poems, he had missed the deadline. Osbert Sitwell wrote to Owen's mother shortly after his death, asking for permission to print Owen's work in the next volume in the series and recommending that a separate collection of his poems should be published. It was Edith Sitwell who selected from manuscripts sent by Owen's mother the seven poems which were eventually included in *Wheels, 1919: A Fourth Cycle* (Oxford: Blackwell, 1919). She also prepared *Poems by Wilfred Owen* for publication, which appeared with a short introduction by Siegfried Sassoon, stressing Owen's selflessness and 'absolute integrity of mind'. Reviews were favourable – John Middleton Murry, writing in *The Nation and Athenæum*, hailed Owen as 'The greatest poet of the war' – but, despite this, sales were relatively poor. The revised edition, published in 1921 and including an extra poem, was also commercially unsuccessful.

p. 53 *Preface*: probably drafted in May 1918 when Owen was making plans to submit a volume of poetry called *Disabled and Other Poems* to Heinemann. Subsequent editors give a slightly different version of his famous remarks on poetry and pity: 'Above all I am not concerned with Poetry. / My subject is War, and the pity of War. / The Poetry is in the pity. / Yet these elegies are in no sense to this generation consolatory.'

p. 54 *Strange Meeting*: first published in *Wheels, 1919*, pp. 52–4. **3 groined:** scooped out.

p. 55 *Another Version*: first published as 'Fragment' in *The Athenæum*, 13 August 1920, p. 201, without the alternative final line supplied here but with the note: 'Wilfred Owen was killed in action on Nov. 4th, 1918.'

p. 56 *Greater Love*: first published in *Art and Letters* III (Spring 1920), p. 6. The title alludes to John 15:13: 'Greater love hath no man than this, that a man lay down his life for a friend.'

p. 57 *Apologia pro Poemate Meo*: The title is Latin for 'apology for my poetry' or 'why I write what I do'. Owen originally called it 'Apologia pro poema mea', but his faulty grammar was corrected by either Sassoon or

Sitwell for this edition. **15 oblation:** a sacrifice or offering to a god. **16 Seraphic:** belonging to the highest order of angels.

p. 59 *The Show*: first published in *Wheels, 1919*, pp. 55–6. **5 plaques:** a medical term used to describe a lesion or patch of eruption on the skin. **20 ramped:** possibly an echo of Laurent Tailhade's pacifist pamphlet *Pour le Paix* (1909): 'Des larves rampent sur le sol', which literally means 'some grubs crawl upon the ground'.

p. 61 *Mental Cases*: first published in *Coterie No. 3* (December 1919), p. 50.

p. 62 *Parable of the Old Men and the Young*: Genesis 22:1–19 recounts the story of how God commands Abraham to sacrifice his son Isaac as a burnt offering. He is about to do so when an angel appears and suggests that he sacrifice a ram instead, thus sparing Isaac's life. Subsequent editors of Owen's poems read *Man* for *Men* in the title, suggesting either a mistranscription on Sitwell's part or, more interestingly, a deliberate alteration on either her or Sassoon's part to make the wartime allegory more obvious.

p. 63 *Arms and the Boy*: first published in *Art and Letters* III (Spring 1920), p. 9. The title is probably an allusion to either George Bernard Shaw's anti-romantic drama about militarism, *Arms and the Man* (1894), or Siegfried Sassoon's poem 'Arms and the Man', published in *The Old Huntsman and Other Poems* (1917).

p. 64 *Anthem for Doomed Youth*: 1 passing-bells: a bell rung immediately after a death to indicate that person's passing. **4 orisons:** prayers. **14 a drawing-down of blinds:** blinds and curtains were traditionally drawn when funeral corteges passed a house or when there had been a death in the household.

p. 66 *Insensibility*: first published in *The Athenæum*, 16 January 1920, p. 71. **3 fleers:** laughs at mockingly or jeers at. **28 cautery:** the medical practice of burning with a hot iron to seal a wound, one side-effect of which might be permanent numbness.

p. 68 *Dulce et Decorum est*: The title, a Latin quote given in full at the end of the poem, is from Horace (65–8 BC). *Odes* III.ii.13. Owen's translation of it, given in a letter to his mother of October 1917, is: 'It is sweet and meet to die for one's country.' **10 clumsy helmets:** gas masks, probably of the Phenate-Hexamine Goggle Helmet variety, which comprised a felt hood with perspex eye-pieces. **25 My friend:** earlier drafts of this poem bear a dedication to Jessie Pope (1868–1941), whose jingoistic rhymes for children were immensely popular during the First World War.

p. 69 *The Sentry*: first published in *Wheels, 1919*, pp. 59–60.

p. 71 *The Dead-Beat*: first published in *Wheels, 1919*, p. 63.

p. 72 *Exposure*: 26 glozed: shone brightly.

p. 76 *The Chances*: first published in *Wheels, 1919*, p. 64.

p. 77 *S.I.W.*: The epigram is from W. B. Yeats's play *The King's Threshold* (1904), first published in *Poems 1899–1905* (1906), p. 238.

p. 79 *Futility*: first published in *The Nation*, 15 June 1918, p. 284. **9 clays:** a poeticism for mankind, possibly echoing Genesis 2:7, where God creates Adam from 'the dust of the earth'. **9 cold star:** the Earth.

p. 80 *Smile, Smile, Smile*: The title is an allusion to 'Pack Up Your Troubles', a popular song much favoured by soldiers during the First World War, which begins: 'Pack up your troubles in your old kit-bag, / And smile, smile, smile.' **2 Yesterday's Mail:** a leading article in the *Daily Mail* for 19 September 1918 referred to society's need to provide decent and comfortable homes for soldiers returning from the war.

p. 82 *A Terre*: first published in *Wheels, 1919*, pp. 57–8. The title is French for 'to earth'. **7 pennies on my eyes:** coins were traditionally placed upon the eyes of the dead to keep them shut. **35 muckman:** a refuse collector. **44 'I shall be one with nature, herb, and stone':** a deliberate misquotation of ll. 370–4 of *Adonais* by the Romantic poet Percy Bysshe Shelley (1792–1822): 'He is made one with Nature . . . / He is a presence to be felt and known / In light and in darkness, from herb and stone'. **50 D'you think the Boche will ever stew man-soup?:** a mocking allusion to one of the more bizarre and persistent rumours of the Great War, that there was a factory behind the German lines for turning corpses into tallow, dubbing and nitro-glycerine.

p. 84 *Wild with all Regrets*: The title is from Tennyson's song, 'Tears, Sweet Tears', in Part IV of *The Princess* (1847): 'Dear as remember'd kisses after death . . . / Deep as first love, and wild with all regret; / O Death in Life, the days that are no more.'

p. 86 *Disabled*: first published in *Wheels, 1919*, pp. 61–2. **2 suit of grey:** wounded soldiers were issued with special grey uniforms to wear whilst convalescing.

p. 88 *The End*: first published in the *Saturday Westminster Gazette*, 15 November 1919, p. 17, and not included in the first edition of *Poems*.

Other Related Poems

Of the five of Owen's poems that appeared during his lifetime, only 'Futility' was included in *Poems by Wilfred Owen*. The four uncollected poems were all later included in Edmund Blunden's *The Poems of Wilfred Owen* (London: Chatto & Windus, 1931) along with 'Asleep', the only new poem by Owen to appear between the publication of the revised edition of Sitwell's text and Blunden's edition.

p. 89 *Song of Songs*: first published in *The Hydra*, 1 September 1917, p. 13, and reprinted in a revised version in *The Bookman*, Vol. LIV, No. 320 (May 1918), p. 52. This was Owen's first published poem. The title is a reference to the biblical Song of Solomon, known as the Song of Songs because of its opening line: 'The song of songs, which is Solomon's.' It is renowned for its overt sensuality.

p. 90 *The Next War*: first published in *The Hydra*, 29 September 1917 and later in *Art & Letters III* (Spring 1920), p. 9. The epigram is the final couplet of Siegfried Sassoon's 'A Letter Home', published in *The Old Huntsman and Other Poems* (1917).

p. 91 *Miners*: first published in *The Nation*, 16 January 1918, p. 539.

p. 93 *Hospital Barge*: first published with 'Futility' in *The Nation*, 15 June 1918, p. 284. **2 Cèrisy:** a village on the Somme Canal in France near Gailly, where Owen was a patient at the 13th Casualty Clearing Station in 1917. **13 Avilon:** the Isle of the Blessed in Celtic mythology and the place to which the mortally wounded King Arthur is taken by barge in the Arthurian legends. **14 Merlin:** the magician at Arthur's court.

p. 94 *Asleep*: first published in *The London Mercury*, Vol. V, No. XIX (May 1921), p. 12, with the note: 'This unpublished poem has been found among Owen's manuscripts by Mr Siegfried Sassoon. Owen was killed on November 4th, 1918, and this poem probably dates from the last few months of his life.'

Glossary of Slang and Military Terms Used by Owen

One direct result of Owen's friendship with Siegfried Sassoon whilst at Craiglockhart and subsequently was that Sassoon encouraged him to abandon his youthful poetic romanticism in favour of a more direct, colloquial style. For ease of reference, the slang and military terms employed by Owen in the poems in this edition are annotated below.

BLIGHTY   soldiers' slang for home or England and also the name given to a wound that ensured a return to Blighty, hence the phrase 'lucky blighter'

BOCHE   like *Fritz* and *the Hun*, soldiers' slang for Germans

BUFFER   an old-fashioned or incompetent person

CRUMP   a 5.9 inch shell, so called because of the noise it made on impact

CUSHY   soldiers' slang for easy or comfortable

DUG-OUT   a roofed shelter dug into the walls of a trench

ESPRIT DE CORPS   a French term meaning team or regimental spirit

FRITZ   see *Boche*

GIDDY JILTS   Scots slang for a capricious young woman

THE HUN   see *Boche*

KNOCKED OUT   see *Pushing up daisies*

LUGGED OUT   carried out or, in this context, to be carried out dead

MESS TINS   small oval buckets which form part of soldiers' cooking and eating utensils

MUSHY   soldiers' slang for emotionally overwrought

PEG   a short alcoholic drink, usually brandy and soda

PEG OUT   see *Pushing up daisies*

PLUCK   courage

PROPS   legs

PUSHING UP DAISIES   like *Knocked out* and *Peg out*, soldiers' slang for dying

SALIENT   the part of the front line closest to enemy territory and thus the most dangerous

SCUPPERED   soldiers' slang for taken prisoner

SHOW   military slang for a battle or operation

SHILLING   the King's shilling, the symbolic payment traditionally given to new recruits to the British army

S.I.W.   military abbreviation for self-inflicted wound

STIFF   soldiers' slang for corpse

STRAFE   a sustained bombardment by rifle or artillery, from the German 'Gott strafe England' – 'God punish England'

TOMMY   the traditional nickname of the British soldier, from the name used in specimen official forms in the early nineteenth century – Thomas Atkins

TRENCH-FOOT   a painful and sometimes fatal affliction of the feet caused by long exposure to damp and cold

Y.M. HUT   Young Men's Christian Association recreation hut, frequently found in larger training and reserve line camps

WHIZZ-BANGS   soldiers' slang for small shells of high velocity, so called because their speed meant that the sound they made in passing through the air was almost simultaneous with their detonation